Plight of the Maven

Maven

ENRICH YOUR
UNDERSTANDING TO
UNLEASH YOUR
SUPER POWERS

Wesley V Crenshaw Jr

Maven Services, LLC.
P.O. Box 836826
Richardson, TX 75083

www.plightofthemaven.com

Ordering Information:
Quantity sales. Special discounts are available on quantity purchases by corporations, associations, and others. For details, contact the publisher at the address above.

3Printed in the United States of America

Maven Services, LLC

ISBN-10: 0615952674
ISBN-13: 978-0615952673

DEDICATION

This book is dedicated to all mavens past, present and future whose problem solving skills have served to the betterment of mankind. The mark of a true maven is how well one attempts to understand the world around them. A true maven sees what is possible by making connections to those things we know and those problems we seek to solve.

And to my lovely wife Vickie, whose endless patience during this process has enabled me to complete this book.

TABLE OF CONTENTS

Table Of Contents

Table Of Contents

Table of Illustrations

Table Of Contents

INTRODUCTION

The book is really to remind us that we
have a way of getting there--we just need
to learn the formula and the system.

Knowledge is power. This statement we have heard many times. It sounds true and, for the most part, it is. It has been used in ways to promote various things. The question is, "Is knowledge really power?"...Since knowledge is having possession of a fact or piece of data, then it has value. So is knowledge just part of the equation? The real challenge to finding out if "knowledge is power" is by looking at the knowledge that we have. What is the knowledge worth? How valuable is it? Does it give you power? Knowledge in and of itself is valuable but not as valuable as the understanding that comes with it. Knowledge without understanding is nothing more than unrelated facts. Knowledge with understanding gives you wisdom. The truer statement would be: "Wisdom Is Power."

This book explores how understanding is derived. It is not enough to simply learn facts. There is an assimilation of facts that gives the understanding we need. It is that power that allows us to unleash the superpowers within us. These superpowers are what could be called executive function. Executive function is the ability to take a task and turn it into a meaningful process. This term is used frequently with people with learning disorders, but the truth is we all benefit from finding ways to increase our executive functions.

Introduction

There is a relationship between emotions and knowledge -- in order to love something, you must have knowledge of the subject. Wine connoisseurs prides themselves in the knowledge they have about wine. Their passion is driven by their knowledge. A car collector finds a love of automobiles from the knowledge about the cars. This will hold true with almost everything. Likewise, the opposite is true. The more we love the subject, the more we want to learn about the subject. I talk about this in the next few chapters. In the path to becoming an expert in a field, we will learn to love the subject. The student who has a genuine interest in the field will be the best student.

The relationship goes even farther in that emotion is the enemy of truth. This happens when we allow our emotions to cloud our judgments about truth. I talk in depth about this in my chapter on biases. This can be one of the biggest challenges we face in all areas of life. Letting our emotions drive our understanding will lead to misunderstanding and confusion.

I talk often about success and what a large part understanding plays in it. We are going to take a journey to success using the path of understanding. Along the way, we will see how others have gained understanding that gave us some of the best technologies mankind has offered. Each one of us has it within us to unleash these techniques; each one of us has the ability to extend our own understanding. Understanding will bring us wisdom in life's journey. Wisdom will bring you success as you define it.

When we look at the technologies that were most disruptive or transformative, we can see these things beginning to emerge. Whether we are talking about the printing press, the internet, or all things in between, we can see the pattern. This pattern is one where technologies build on each other. Each technology comes from the desire to solve a problem. While solving a single problem a stepping stone to another technology is created. One of the most transformative technologies mankind has created is the integrated circuit. To most people, while they have heard of this, they may not understand its impact. The integrated circuit was not possible without the semiconductor, and the microprocessor was not possible without the integrated circuit. In a simpler time the printing press relied on moving type to be successful, but the moving type relied on lead molding to be possible. So you see from just two examples how the most transformative technologies relied on other technologies. The reach and impact of these discoveries could not possibly be understood by their creators.

So, why read this book? Why this subject? The answer could not be clearer: if we are to understand and extend our capabilities, our technologies, we must learn how it's been done in the past. We must learn from those who have done these things, what it was and how they did them? What were the traits and habits that they employed in order to create transformative success?

As you go through this book, you will start to realize that some of these things may be reasonably commonsense, some of these things you will already know, and you may not have realized most of these points all work together. The book is really to remind us that we have a way of getting there--we just need to learn the formula and the system.

Introduction

CHAPTER 1 - WHAT IS A MAVEN?

Knowledge is meaningless without understanding.

Our road to success must be founded on a primary goal. This success we are seeking will be based on the strength of understanding. Our plight, or challenge, is to become an expert or a "maven." Our success relies heavily on our expertise of the subject. We will never be able to become a true expert or "maven" until we have mastered the understanding of the subject we are seeking to perfect. Success will be the outcome. Along the road we are taking we are creating an understanding of a success system, how to identify it and how to create our own. Our road will have many challenges along the way. If we are to build a strong success system we will have to ensure we get the outcomes we are expecting, for knowledge is meaningless without understanding. Without understanding, knowledge is just a collection of unrelated facts. So our plight or the plight of the maven is to reach a level of understanding where problems seem to solve themselves-- an understanding which makes working a vocation seem like a natural gift.

The word maven

Maven is not a word we use very often these days...you may not have even heard it before. It comes from the Hebrew "mevin", or "one who understands." A maven is simply an expert, someone you refer to as a guru, a master or a mentor. The definition has several layers but at the simplest, a maven is one who understands at a level deeper than others. A maven is someone who has a deep understanding of a subject. When you need someone an answer or insight that is not apparent to most people, you can consult a guru, a master, a mentor or a maven. A maven is a collector of information. A maven finds connections in information. A maven assimilates the information into understanding. Mavens never stop learning and is willing to pass on the knowledge they have to others. A maven is a go-to person. A maven is always trying to work out how to solve problems or design something better. Mavens walk around with ideas in their head, go to sleep at night with these ideas and wake up in the morning with these ideas. Mavens will work through numerous issues before coming to a solution. As you learn how this works and begin to practice these things, you too will be able to do the same things.

Mavens are perpetual problem solvers, but it's not because they like the problems. Mavens are looking for the solution because they want to avoid problems and want things to work better. Many people would consider the maven to be a genius. A maven might score high on IQ tests, but it has more to do with the way a maven approaches solving problems and learning than sheer intellect. It is not a requirement to have a high IQ to be a maven, but practicing the same principles will give you the ability to score high on IQ tests. In this book, I will expose those traits and lessons on how anyone can become a maven in any area of study, competency, skill, proficiency or craft.

This is a learning system

This book is intended as a success system that will be useful to you in any enterprise you choose. To make this point clearer, this is not a teaching system. This is a learning system that you will use to extract the most useful information from courses, books, DVDs or other learning materials. Once you learn how this system works and begin to practice the traits and methods, you will find it easier to become a maven with new skill sets.

Once you decide to take on a new subject you may ask yourself, "How hard is that going to be for me to learn this?" Oftentimes we convince ourselves that the process will be much more difficult than it should be. Just because you have never studied the subject before does not mean that you will not be able to pick it up quickly and easily.

I will start by asking you this question, "What are you going to do to learn this material?" "How do you approach learning new materials?" This sounds like a simple query, but as you will find, there is a system of things you can do to extract the information needed to build a deep understanding of the subject or field we are learning. We are not talking about just learning a subject; we are talking about becoming an expert in it. The person who writes courses or creates lesson plans wants to present the materials in a certain way. Sometimes the materials are not presented in the most efficient way for some to learn. Since we retain such a small amount of the information that we are being taught, it is incumbent upon us to learn a more efficient way to learn the materials. By using the traits and habits I outline along with some constructs that you will learn to identify, you will absorb the learning materials much more thoroughly.

What will you learn?

You will learn the building blocks to becoming a maven, and you will also discover that knowledge is transferable between competencies. Once you learn to identify these transferable skills, you can use the skills to become a maven in multiple competencies. There are significant benefits to you beyond just being a maven for a single competency, too. The more you can expand your universe of knowledge the easier it becomes to become a maven in other fields. You will become less reliant on others and more empowered to do things yourself. You will lose the fear associated with taking on projects you have never attempted before. It is my desire that you learn the skills that will allow you to adapt to an ever changing world.

Who benefits from this book?

This book will serve as a road map for those who are already mavens in at least one craft and are looking to repeat this in other areas. Who benefits most from this book?

- If you have a career that requires you to "get up to speed" quickly, these tools will be very helpful as well.

- If you are just starting out in a career and you want to excel in your field, this book will definitely help you.

- If you are a parent and want to pass some skills to your teenage children, this book would be a great gift to them.

- If you are a professional in a career that demands you have subject matter expertise in many other areas of study, this is a book for you.

- This book is really for anyone who has the desire to reach for the higher levels of his or her profession.

With these skills your friends, family and co-workers will begin to seek you out for help, advice and begin to respect your opinions as informed. There are a number of opportunities that will result from this learning skill. Many of my friends may consider me a maven for several reasons. I am one of those people who scores high on IQ tests and can pick up areas of expertise quickly. Here are a few examples of areas where I have a high level of expertise: carpentry, home repairs, electrical matters, plumbing, automobile mechanics, tool and die making, machining, automotive painting and body work, fabrication, manufacturing processes, CNC programming, computer networking, computer systems management, automation development, web technologies, virtualization, cooking/culinary skills, systems integration - and the list grows all the time. For many of my family and friends I am "Mr. Fixit." My interests are also in stock market trading, investing, real estate and even the political environment. It seems daily I get involved in helping people solve a whole variety of problems. While the scope of this book is about developing the traits necessary to become an expert or a maven, anyone can practice the skills I outline in this book for everyday living.

How do we find that competency?

Learning a competency comes from our own personal

interest in a subject. It could be the result of exposure at an early age, family tradition, opportunities or just a fondness for a particular subject. *Finding the love of the subject is the most powerful driver you can have for learning the subject.*

For many people, learning a new craft is challenging, but it does not have to be. If you do not like the subject, this process becomes incredibly difficult. It is vitally important to find a motivation to learn the subject. The motivation for learning will come from within more than from outside. When I ask young people what they want to do as a career, many have no idea. Some of these subjects will not come to them until they are faced with a career opportunity or a relationship which drives them in a given direction. It is my hope that a young person reading this book will find the confidence to approach an area of study with the expectation of being able to learn and acquire the necessary skills. It is not essential that you know all you want to do; you just need to know you have the skills necessary to learn whatever you need to succeed.

Find a way to love the subject by finding early victories and then build on those victories. Nothing is more discouraging than to try to learn something only to have one obstacle after another keep getting in your way. Small victories are the key to confidence building. When you focus too much on the failures, your attitude will suffer. You find a way to focus on the victories in order to build your attitude and confidence. Your confidence will make the subject more approachable. As you build your confidence, your drive will increase. Before long, you will begin to want to take on more and more of the subject until you realize you have become an expert.

So in order to find victories we must define what a victory is. For an entertainer, applause is reinforcement. For a chef watching people delight in a meal will be a victory. A victory is anything that our actions produce that has value to others. Another example would be when a programmer solves a problem with a program. Comedians may start out by getting laughs from their family, but to build on those victories they try to get laughs from friends, then strangers. When one approach fails, they try another until the desired results are achieved. It's their love for laughter that drives them to be a better comedian. The lesson in this is to learn to love the subject you're taking on. Your drive is based on victories at an early point. If this is making sense, then this point is going to be a powerful one. The point is that you will want to find the "art" in every subject you take on. The art will then give you the gratification of a job well done. The art is where we find our creative spirit. Creativity is what separates us from robots that may be doing the same task.

Some of man's greatest discoveries and innovations came from individuals who had a desire to reach an outcome. These desires were focused in such a way that the individual would have to operate outside the common system in order to achieve his or her goals. Taking on a subject because it has a high earning potential may hinder our efforts. If you are never able to achieve a desire to know and understand the subject, this will turn the learning of the subject into an exercise rather than a journey of purpose. Each subject we approach should be treated as we treat a hobby.

The things that you learn in this book must be practiced. Everything you do benefits from the things that you can learn in this book and put into practice. You will want to begin practicing these things at every opportunity you can. If you take a class on a particular subject and you only practice that subject while in class, you will not gain a deep understanding. You should want to practice the subject; it should be something you focus on, even when it is not required.

CALL TO ACTION:

Find an area of study you would like to learn. Find a way to become passionate about wanting to learn it.

NOTES:

_____

CHAPTER 2 - EMPOWERING YOURSELF

It takes no special skills to be poor or powerless.
In fact, it is so easy that many people get there
without even trying

We will face obstacles to our goals along the way. This is to be expected. Our goals can be accomplished with the way we empower ourselves. Empowerment is a very strong motivator; it is the reason we take on new subjects in the first place.

Creating options

In order to understand about empowerment, we have to understand the nature of empowerment. People who have power over their own lives are people who have options. In any situation if you can give yourself options, you have choices. Options give you better choices; better choices give you more control, and more control gives you power. It is the people who feel they have no control over their lives who are powerless. By becoming a maven and especially a maven in multiple fields of study, you will provide yourself with many options. The motive of creating options for oneself should be front and center in every situation you encounter in life.

We are attracted to survival stories because inevitably there is a hero who seems to have the right answer. This hero generally possesses instinctive survival skills. The hero of the story looks at the situation and begins to find ways to gain options such as finding shelter or building shelter, how to get food and other essentials. Those are the first priorities. The others in the story sit helplessly by and wait for help or cannot figure out the next move. A hero will figure out options and try to create more options, therefore, giving more power to the hero and the group at large.

I start with this lesson or concept not because it is part of the process of becoming a maven; it is the driving force or motive for doing it. Gaining power over one's life is inborn in us, it is our survival instinct. This ability is not to be confused with those who strive to gain power over others' lives. That would be using your superpowers for evil, and I am not advocating that.

Dealing with stressful situations

Have you ever noticed how everyone deals with stress differently? There have been studies with small children who were put in a small room with only a gate blocking them in. The scientists observed the children becoming stressed about not being able to escape, and as they watched the children, it was apparent that even as children, we all approach problems or obstacles differently. Apparently, we are pre-wired with a set of responses. In at least one of the examples, the child simply sits by the gate and loudly cries out in protest. In several of the other examples, the children stand next to the gate holding on as they're waiting for an adult to set them free. Other examples showed the children's attempts to scale the gate in an effort to escape on their own. Here we see the survivalist spirit finds a way to overcome the current situation by creating options. The gated children studies illustrate that problems are by and large perceived, meaning that we interpret things to be problems even when they may not be at all.

Having problems is not the problem. Having problems gives us direction. Failure is a part of success, and problems are inherent in anything we do. In many instances, I have later found that the problems I encountered served as a blessing in that they forced me to find the best solution. Learning not to allow problems to stop us, but rather letting them teach us how to overcome those problems hones our skills as long as we use them for later problem solving opportunities. Encountering problems shows us where our solution can be enhanced and allows for better system design.

During a crisis, people often will not respond but rather wait out the crisis hoping things will get better on their own. These people have what is called a *"normalcy bias."* Most people fall into that group. However, a maven will analyze the situation and make decisions based on available information and react accordingly. If you want to be a maven, you must learn the virtue of putting stress aside and overcome problems by being the most informed person in the room. You examine your environment, seeking those things that will help you achieve a goal and are able to recognize the tools that can be useful even when a path forward is not evident. The first priority is always to find more options; the best solution will often present itself.

I want to share a true story with you. The lesson is an example of how we make more options for ourselves. One day, I got a call from my adult age son.

He is 200 miles away from me, and he is in an almost

panic situation. He is 25 miles from his house travelling with his wife and baby son. The car he is driving has overheated, and he had to stop at a car repair shop. If you have ever faced a situation when your car was overheating and your child was crying, you can easily see how stressful that can be. The repair shop told him that his radiator had a leak in it, and it was not repairable. It needed to be replaced. The shop wanted to charge him somewhere in the neighborhood of $250 to replace the radiator. His question to me was whether he should let them replace it and take the financial hit. The reason it overheated was a lack of coolant. So, we have what appears to be coolant loss due to a leak.

The shop told him the type of radiator he had was not able to be patched. He was calling me because he felt that he was in a situation where he had few options. He felt powerless over the situation and was seeking some advice.

Sometimes it helps to consult someone else when the situation is too stressful. Getting someone else's ideas will allow us to break out of the biases we form about the situation. My advice to him was simply this: Get more options. I advised him to fill the radiator with water and drive straight home, and if the engine temperature began to rise too high, pull over and put more water in it. The goal was to reach the house.

The logic was that once he reached his house, he then would have more options; his wife and child were safe, and he could make a better decision about how to fix the problem without the added stress the situation was placing on him. My son took my advice and made it all the way home without another issue. In fact, he drove the car for another two weeks before he decided to address the problem. He was able to solve the problem on his schedule because he took power back in the situation and was in control instead of letting the situation control him. He then had the skills and the means: He had learned some basic mechanical skills, had his tools and had time to get the best price on parts and a place to fix the car. What he was able to do is the same thing almost anyone else could have done. Because he had taken time to learn some basic skills and acquire some tools, he was able to take control because he had created options for himself even in a stressful situation.

Another situation similar to this happened to my neighbor. She was a single mom and possessed little in the way of mechanical skills, mechanical knowledge or tools. She was totally dependent on others for help in these matters. She came outside to find a flat tire on her only vehicle. She told me that she would have to call a tow truck and have her car towed to the tire shop where she would have the tire replaced. In her mind, this was her only option. She was never one to consider all the options; she was very dependent on others, and she was powerless. After I explained to her that it was probably a simple puncture that could be repaired easily and reliably, she was somewhat relieved. I went to my tool box where I keep a plug kit (which only costs a few dollars and will fix several holes) and was able to fix the tire. I plugged her tire and told her that as long as it didn't have a slow leak, she would be able to drive on it for as long as needed. Here is a situation where I offered an option of which she was not aware. The tire never developed a slow leak, and she continued to drive on that tire.

As a younger man, I found myself in situations like this.

I learned to overcome the situations by leveraging what I had around me. I never allowed the stress of the situation to cloud my thoughts. I remember fixing a flat with nothing more than a screwdriver, a pair of pliers, a can of "Fix-A-Flat" and a shoe string.

In another situation, I was able to repair a broken accelerator cable by rigging a handle and rerouting the cable to get some functionality out of it. Some of the ideas may seem crazy at the time, but remember our goal is to get to a place where we have the control, options and ability to make better decisions.

Locus of Control

People who feel that the things that happen in their lives are outside of their control or the world is out to get them, is said to have an *EXTERNAL LOCUS OF CONTROL* (ELOC). People who are like this generally do not know how to create their own options.

They are the ones who demand that everyone else solve their problems. They are the most easily enslaved into a job or a situation because they believe they are powerless to change anything. A person who has an ELOC is easily manipulated by those who appear to have the individual's best interest in mind, but rarely do. It is very hard for people who do not have options or feel that they do not have options, to change their station in life. They generally pass this mindset to their children by their words and actions, and the problems can be perpetuated generation after generation.

If you feel that you may have an ELOC, this book should be of particular help. It should not discourage you, but teach you the things that you should concentrate on and serve as a light in the darkness, a beacon of enlightenment. In fact, I would challenge you to find a young person you know who has an ELOC and see if you can change his or her life too. You should find an accountability partner and share what you learn and encourage each other. It frequently helps to see things through the eyes of others simply because of our own biases. If we as individuals can become more empowered, then we as a society will benefit greatly.

It takes no special skills to be poor or powerless. In fact, it is so easy that many people get there without even trying. Not setting priorities and poor buying habits cause people to make bad financial decisions.

I want to share a story about a friend of mine. His name is Benny. We have been friends since we were young. Benny is a classic example of a person who has an ELOC view. Benny has no real education; he was passed along in school due to a learning disorder. Benny allows life to control him, and he would view success very differently than I do. Benny is a powerless person who works low-paying, dead end jobs. He is very hard to employ because he lacks the ability to solve problems. He spends every dollar he gets almost as soon as he gets it. He has no future prospects of changing his station in life.

Control your family's finances! I have seen too many examples of where the inability to control spending has caused many families to live as slaves to their jobs. Just because you have a good job is not a justification to spend everything you make when or before you make it. Having financial means gives you options like no other.

People with an *INTERNAL LOCUS OF CONTROL*

(ILOC) are people who feel that they do have control over their lives. They are the ones who will take risks and benefit from them. People who have an ILOC are more likely to be a leader. They will be the type of

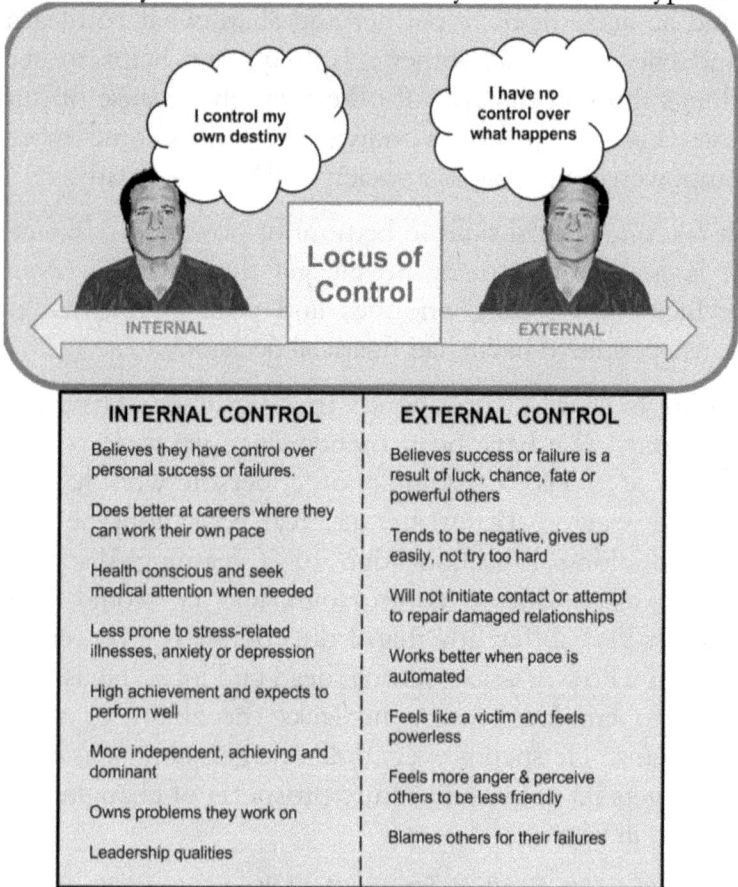

INTERNAL CONTROL	EXTERNAL CONTROL
Believes they have control over personal success or failures.	Believes success or failure is a result of luck, chance, fate or powerful others
Does better at careers where they can work their own pace	Tends to be negative, gives up easily, not try too hard
Health conscious and seek medical attention when needed	Will not initiate contact or attempt to repair damaged relationships
Less prone to stress-related illnesses, anxiety or depression	Works better when pace is automated
High achievement and expects to perform well	Feels like a victim and feels powerless
More independent, achieving and dominant	Feels more anger & perceive others to be less friendly
Owns problems they work on	Blames others for their failures
Leadership qualities	

Figure 1 Locus of Control

individual who will elevate themselves to be a maven. If you feel that you are this type of person, this book will be of a special value to you, too, because you will more quickly reap the benefits. You will start applying the lessons right away. ILOC people already understand the power of having options, even if they never stopped and considered it exactly in those terms.

The power of owning tools

Tools are an important part of being a maven, so do not be afraid to own tools. Tools come in many forms. There are tools for automotive repair, household repairs, software tools and the skills you learn from this book, which are tools in and of themselves. A person with tools has options and options are the root of empowerment. When you become a person who can use tools to create tools, you now have an infinite power. Everything we use is either a tool or a toy. If you squander your wealth on toys instead of tools, you will be missing out on all the benefits tools will give you. Some things are both tools and toys. The difference has everything to do with the context by which they are used. Children use tools as toys; men use tools as tools.

Your family PC is a classic example of this. If all you do is play games, then it is a toy. If you use it for something productive, it is a tool. So, if you are saying to yourself, "I cannot afford to buy tools," consider this: If you pay someone to do something for you, you are paying for his or her tools. Often, you can pay for most tools with a single use or sometimes the second time you use the tool. This approach makes affording tools much easier. I have a philosophy about buying tools: Buy a less expensive tool if you feel that you may not use it that often. This will protect you from over investing in tools you won't use. Less expensive tools are more prone to failing, however. If you find that you use the less expensive tool enough to wear it out or cause it to fail, then you can rationalize buying a better one. This approach allows you to own a larger variety of tools rather than a small number of expensive tools. A small business gives a lot of thought to buying its first fax machine, but as the business becomes dependent on the fax machine, buying its replacement is not a hard decision because it is essential.

Let's revisit our situation where we have people in a survival situation. Now that it has been established that they may be there for a while, the hero of our story now sends other members of the party to begin taking inventory of all the island has to offer. He sends them out to find out what resources can be utilized. Knowing full well that tools are important as well as other necessities, he begins to plan so that he can create the things needed, such as more permanent shelter and the production of other tools. In his mind, he knows that building materials will be the most important next step. It is his goal to figure out how he can produce twine from fibrous plants indigenous to the island. If he has to cultivate them to make them more abundant, this would be part of his plan. With the ability to produce a twine, he now can produce a variety of products needed by the survivors. A twine can be used to produce rope, and the rope would then be a basic building material for things such as fishing nets, thatched roofs for huts, bridges, hand tools and even weapons such as bows for arrows, ladders and the list goes on and on. If he wanted, he could even weave it together to make canvas for bags or clothing. Fiber is one of the single most important materials for most building products. He could find binding materials in plant resins or natural tar pits to use to create a whole new variety of other materials. Early civilizations would put straw in clay to produce bricks.

So for our hero knowing that being able to produce fibrous materials would create the most options for any other products the group would need to survive. The list of possibilities becomes almost limitless. The fact that the spent fiber products could then be burned for fuel makes this exercise all the more important. After it is all said and done, all we are doing in this whole exercise is giving you the tools to build the tools you need to conquer the challenges that you will face throughout your life. We talk about the empowerment of tools and resources because those things can be leveraged. Survival is a powerful motivator, and in order to be a survivor, you will want to have the capabilities of a maven. If you are someone who considers yourself to be a survivalist, being able to learn new skills is a tool.

Throughout this book my goal is to teach you about empowerment. Empowerment is the mission of the maven or his plight. In later chapters, I will be talking about systems. As we explore systems, keep in mind that we are looking for empowerment through options. A well designed system will allow you to create your own options, which is at the heart of empowerment. Since we consider tools to be an important part of creating options, we have to view all things as tools.

CALL TO ACTION:

Look for a situation in your life where you feel that you have few options. Take out a piece of paper and write down a list of options you would like to have. Then, for each option, consider what conditions would have to exist for those options to be available. After you have a list of conditions, create a mission statement for each.

NOTES:

What changes if any, could you make to become more ILOC?

Are there ways to create options in your job or in your home life?

Make a list of tools that you should own to give yourself better options and choices.

CHAPTER 3 - TURNING LEMONS INTO LEMONADE

*I was determined not to allow this situation to
permanently disable my self-esteem.*

I grew up in a very small town. Like many small towns,
it was in an agricultural community. We lived far enough
away from most things that if we needed to get
something done, we usually had to find a way to do it
ourselves. We didn't have access to services that people
in town had. If we had a problem with a vehicle, we
found a way to fix it. If we needed something built, we
built it. If we needed a tool, we fabricated it, or we knew
someone who could. As a teenager of 14, I went to
work in the local auto parts store as my first job. We
sold parts for cars, trucks and tractors, and we were the
only parts store for miles so we got to know everyone in
town. We had to know about things from older cars to
newer cars to tractors. We were asked daily our advice
on how to fix the vehicles we sold parts for.

My plight as a teenager

Being a young teenager surrounded by older men, I
found myself the subject of a lot of ridicule and
belittling. I could count on a fair amount of criticism
and harassment on a daily basis. This was not due to my
lack of intellect; some of the "baiting" was because of
my naiveté, but most of it was they were having fun at
my expense.

It became more to do with a gang-like mentality that
occurs when a person is singled out from the pack for

ridicule. Today we might call this bullying. Many people cannot deal well with this kind of stress, and it will cause some lasting emotional scars. I was called stupid and worthless on many occasions; the other workers would use me as the brunt of their jokes. Since the local parts store was also a hangout for some of the locals, many times the friends of my coworkers would engage in the ridicule, as well. Like I said, it was a gang-like pack mentality.

This was my first real job, and I didn't want to simply quit, but on the other hand, I was powerless to stop the bullying. The whole experience for me was both a blessing and a curse. The curse was that it did affect my self-esteem in a way that caused me to doubt myself. However, the parts store also had its blessings. I got exposure to a lot of information about automobiles, tractors and even motorcycles. We rebuilt engines for ourselves in the back of the shop, and we machined brake parts. Being the low man on the totem pole, many of these tasks fell on me. In fact, I ran the counter, turned brake drums and rotors, checked in parts, restocked the shelves and even mowed the grass outside the store. I learned to wear many hats at a very young age.

My path begins in the face of a challenge

The daily exposure began to take a toll. This created a struggle or plight for me. On one hand, they were teaching me many things about the auto parts business. We raced motorcycles on the weekends, and in many ways the men were friends to me. On the other hand, I had to deal with the stress of all the ridicule. My plight was to find my worth by honing my skills while I was there. Oftentimes, I would walk the shelves, pulling parts out of boxes and examining them, studying them, memorizing part numbers. I would study the parts catalogs. I would find the parts that would fit a variety of cars, which cars shared similar parts, look at the way the part numbers related to the various parts. I got to the point where I could not only recognize what each part was, but also determine the make and a year range of the vehicles they would fit. I got so good at it that at times I was able to walk to the shelf and pull the part without asking the customer any information about the car they were working on. I found this most helpful when a husband, working on his car, would send his wife to the parts store, and she would not know what she was after. She just brought the part in with her. This happens a lot when you are in the middle of the job, and you don't want to clean up just to make a parts run. It gave me a sense of accomplishment that drove me to be better.

When working in that store, I was doing something I was not aware of at the time, learning the system of identifying parts and associating them with the part number. Later in my life, I would come to recognize this ability as a trait of a maven. (I will talk about this later in the chapter about systems.) In all this experience, the true blessing came in the form of how I dealt with the situation. I was determined not to allow this situation to permanently disable my self-esteem. In the process, I developed skills that would carry me to become a maven, in many competencies. I was an internal control person in an external situation and by honing my skills, I was able to give myself the options to overcome my current station.

One of the negative side effects of all this was that I was very quick to try to show my worth by becoming a person who many would try to characterize as a "know-it-all." This was merely my attempt to show my worth to the outside world, which up to this time did not seem at all interested in my worth. People who are trying to overcome self-esteem issues will often resort to these tactics. A little bit of knowledge was treated as a tool to show the world I had value. I have noticed this trait in others; while the world would think they are prideful or boastful, what they are really trying to do is find their own worth by forcing the world to find value in them. I found myself again having to adjust my personality to be a bit more palatable to others.

The struggle of many mavens

This is where many people who strive to be mavens struggle. On one hand, you see knowledge and the value in gathering the knowledge, yet on the other hand, sharing the knowledge becomes a skill that has to be honed. I can tell you it took me years before I would be able to fully comprehend what was really happening to me. The owner of the parts store was an alcoholic, so drinking was prevalent during my time there. My co-workers would often drink while at work. I felt that was a huge catalyst for the experience I was having there. I was not much of a drinker; I would occasionally have a beer, but I was not old enough to drink, and it just simply did not appeal to me. Many years later as an adult I had the privilege to talk with my former boss, and it was great to talk to him. He was a reformed alcoholic by this time, and he felt that he owed me an apology for the experience I had at his shop. By then, I was able to explain that I was an accomplished computer programmer, designing automation systems for a very large Fortune 100 company. I said that it was the very ridicule that he apologized for that drove me to learn and hone my skills.

It was my attempt to show my own self-worth that pushed me to develop the skills necessary to learn how to learn. I became a product of my environment. Instead of allowing it to have a negative impact, I turned it into a positive by creating my own options, not allowing the stress to stifle me and treating the problem as something I needed to overcome. Each one of us must find the drive we need to learn a skill. We are all different in how that will happen. For some, the decision to learn a new skill may be an easy one while for others the pressure of a situation may force them to.

Some of us decide on a subject because we have an interest in the subject. For others, it has as much to do with the skills they may already possess. A person who good with math or can grasp technical concepts, may be drawn to a field in engineering or one of the sciences. If you are a creative person, you will look for fields where you can express your own creativity. We cannot create these intangibles. What we can do, however, is to understand that with each type of skill, we can nurture the habits and traits that will allow us to get the best out of them.

CALL TO ACTION:

Find out what drives you. Each one of us has different interests, strengths and weaknesses. Look for your strengths and try to leverage them. Find what you are passionate about and understand why. Your passions will change over time as your skills improve.

NOTES:

List some challenges in your life which affected your attitude in a positive way.

List some challenges in your life which possibly changed your personality, how did you recognize the changes?

Can you think of some things that you could do differently in the future?

CHAPTER 4 - FIND THE SYSTEM

*The challenge each time you find a working system
is to sit down and identify the formula.*

On our road to success we have to become familiar with the concept of systems and how they build the world around us. We are going to try to understand how systems work.

Learning how to identify a system will give you an edge on learning the behaviors of that particular competency. Understanding the nature and principles of each system gives us the authority to become experts in that competency. Once you can identify a system, you will be able to fit the pieces into the system to reach a new, deeper level of understanding, and this is the essence of being a maven.

At the core of the system is a formula. We can examine nature to learn its systems. In all things there is a system. Humans also have systems.

→ If you are in sales there's a system.

→ In your computers there's a system.

→ If you're in carpentry there's a system.

→ If you're an automobile mechanic, the art of diagnosing a problem with your car is something that some mechanics do better than others. Why? You guessed it--they have a system.

→ If you're going to be a cook or chef, there is a system.

→ If you're going to be an accountant, there is a system.

→ If you're going to be a stock trader, there are numerous systems.

→ Becoming a doctor involves learning a system.

→ Business models follow systems, as well.

All Governments, cultures, businesses, TV shows, novels, etc. have systems. There is always a system. Computer programmers such as myself understand this concept. Any time we start to solve a problem using the computer, we must develop an algorithm that will become our program. An algorithm is a fancy name for steps to solve the problem with a formula. Our computer program then must follow a strategy with each time the program runs. So, we now have a system based on a formula, algorithm or strategy.

Success systems utilize a formula

Since our road leads to success, we have to find and build a success system. At the core of our formula we have a strategy or algorithm. A strategy is based on a set of rules. There are rules for mathematical formulas, so shall there be rules for a success formula. The rules in a strategy are designed to keep our biases out of decision making. If we have a solid set of rules, our strategy will have a high degree of successful outcomes. We can observe businesses who are successful and compare them to similar businesses who are not successful. The differences may be subtle, but the outcomes are vastly different. The strategy will be different. A strategic difference may be the market these businesses target or the way they advertise. There is always a difference, and you will learn to find the differences. Modeling your system after a success formula or success system will make the difference. Many businesses exist for years without growth even though they follow a system that may have been successful at one time or another. Markets change, and, therefore, the strategy and system should change along with it.

Learn to identify the formula

As you watch TV, you can identify the formula or system the writers use to create situation comedies. They change slightly over time, but the basic premise is always the same. Likewise with a crime drama, the basic layout of each story is similar. There are systems to attract certain types of audiences whether they are male, female, old, young, and of various ethnicities and so forth.

The formula or system used many times in detective shows is one similar to this. The show is centered around a key person, who is the maven. The maven has a supporting cast made up of at least a woman and a man. There is some chemistry either implied or deliberate between them. The mavens have a unique skill that gives him or her the ability to solve the problem. The show moves through the story line with obvious clues and obstacles. These clues and obstacles create pieces to the puzzle. The clues lead you in various directions until almost the end of the episode. A different character will say or do something that will trigger the maven to a solution. The story ends with all the pieces neatly in place. The misdirection of the story line are designed to confuse and frustrate the audience. This causes the audience to become emotionally invested in the outcome. This formula can be found in numerous popular TV series. The formula works. The differences between the stories are based on subject matter, locations, names, skills and time, but the basic formula still remains.

Popular music follows a formula. The songs have a basic set of chords that are arranged in a series of repeating patterns with an interruption in the pattern past the halfway point. Then, the pattern is again repeated. The lyrics follow a similar pattern with the chorus thrown in at intervals to keep the music patterns moving.

People who can seek out these systems by identifying the formula will find themselves not only able to apply these systems in certain areas, but also to take the format or the formula to other systems. The important thing to note is that success has a system whether it's music, TV or business. By identifying the success formula or system, you can use the system to gain your own success. The road to success requires this understanding.

Using systems to solve problems

As we analyze a system, we have to understand that the system is built upon processes or methods. Methods are used to create the formula. The formula is what the system operates on. Therefore, a system is a series of methods that combine to produce a single task. Larger systems are built from a series of smaller systems or sub-systems.

We think of math when we think of formulas, but consider that math simply uses formulas. A formula can be any group of processes or methods in which you follow a prescribed set of rules for each strategy.

A math example: We want to find the number of gallons in a pipe. We use a formula to calculate the volume of a cylinder, we then multiply that volume by a factor to convert the cubic inches/centimeters to gallons, and then we add to the formula to create a new formula. The process is the same formula if we are calculating the number of gallons in a barrel, drum or pipe. If we are finding the number of gallons in a box, we only modify our formula slightly. In this case, the method is to find the cubic volume first then convert the units to gallons. The system works because it is a proven system. In physics, we have a number of formulas and the system for using most calculations in physics involves converting all the units to the same prior to doing the calculation. This is a rule. The methods for using math formulas are established by mathematical principles and laws of mathematics.

Accounting systems are based on GAAP or Generally Accepted Accounting Principles. If you are building an accounting system, you will need to understand how these principles fit. The formula is based on a dual entry method where the currency cannot go into a new account without first leaving another account. This system was designed to make all things accountable. The reason it works so well is because it can control the entry points and exit points for currency or value within the system. It gives the entity an accurate picture of the flow of currency throughout the system. In other words, all things must come back to zero. It uses the concept of debits and credits (plus and minus) to achieve the results. There should be as many debits as there are credits for the system to be in balance.

In the parts store, we had a number of systems. Every manufacturer had a system of numbering. Once I was able to figure out each one's system, my job as a parts person became much easier. I remember on one occasion when I was visiting another parts store. A customer came in with a part that the counter guy did not recognize. It was a ballast resistor that older cars and trucks used on their ignition systems. The counter person looked at his manager as if to say, "Would we even have such a thing?" I recognized the part from my memorization exercises and knew basically what the part number was. As both the counter person and the manager wondered what to do, I quickly responded and asked the customer, "Is that a six volt or twelve volt system?" Then I asked the store manager, "Which brand of ignition parts do you carry?" He responded, "Standard ignition." I looked at the counter person and said, "The part number is an RU-10." He looked at the manager, and the manager shrugged his shoulders and said, "Try it." He went to the shelf and came back with the box. He opened it to find it was an exact match. You see, in this situation, I had memorized what these parts looked like and what they were called, so all I had to do then was understand the numbering system to identify the exact part needed. The "RU" prefix told me that it was a resistor block, and the number "10" told me it was in the twelve volt range. I knew which numbers the brand standard ignition normally used. It was just a matter of connecting the dots.

Systems are made up of sub-systems

As a maven, you may develop many systems, depending upon your area of study. Each time you develop a system, you will apply a formula that you have created for dealing with different types of situations.

The challenge each time you find a working system is to sit down and identify the formula. A system that is used to support a larger system is called a sub-system. Later in the chapter on layers, this concept will be explored much more in depth. Think about your family automobile as an example. It is a large system which is used for transportation, but the larger system is supported by numerous sub-systems. All the sub-systems do their tasks but work together for the larger system to do its task.

Understanding why systems do what they do and how to apply them is what mavens do instinctively. Learning to identify formulas within systems gives you an advantage when looking for solutions to problems. We are making our systems transferable. You can borrow from an existing system to enhance another system. If you find that your system may have an inefficiency, borrowing concepts from other efficient systems can give you a platform for enhancement.

Know what the solution looks like in order to solve the problem

Whatever you set out to do, keep in mind that the first order of business is to SOLVE THE PROBLEM. Too many times we get caught up in details that are unrelated, and we fail because we are not clear on what the real goal is. When I start to solve a problem, the first thing I do is define the results. This is where most people struggle. We see it all the time--the process becomes the focus, and the problem never gets resolved. The results may be nothing more than "a solution that works." If you leave this as a broad definition, you don't get trapped into a single line of thinking. A solution that works needs to be understood based on how "works" is defined.

For example, often, people bring me a project and tell me what they think they want. Several times after drilling down into the problem, I find that what they want is not a function of what they need. If we attack the problem from the position of "what will make this work," the solution may look different than what they think they want. On one occasion, I had a manager ask me to write a report based on a set of fields he had determined. I asked questions about the format and such things. I even offered to include additional information that would help the report. After I found out he was going to simply take the data from the report I created and manually type it into a spreadsheet that he created, I suggested that we might want to take a different approach. He assumed that there was no way to get the data from one source and put it into the spreadsheet without a lot of manual work.

I asked him if I could automate the process so that he could make the whole thing seamless. He agreed. I created a spreadsheet that was a blank with headers and some macros to import the data. Instead of creating a report, I dumped the formatted data to a file. All he had to do was execute the report on one system to create the data file and then execute the macro in the spreadsheet and within a second he had what he really needed.

He was planning on running the report once a month

because he didn't feel that he had time to manually enter the data. I gave the power to execute it multiple times a day, if needed. He was very excited because this empowered him.

In our story, we have several things happening. First, I gave him options that he did not think he had. Next, I created a process that would involve only a few steps. The system I used was based on a formula I had used many times before: Use the general ledger accounting program to produce a text output which other tools could then use. By leveraging an existing system, you will be able to apply the formulas that make up that system to other systems.

Not all systems are efficient

Engineers have always used systems that they have observed in nature to create new systems. A proven and well-designed system will always work. Many systems that we see in our world are not based on a well-designed platform. These systems become increasingly complicated and fail to solve the most basic of goals. We often will throw resources at the system, believing that we can achieve the goals. The system begins to collapse under its own weight. Systems like these are not based on a proven formula. As a maven, you too will be able to identify these systems. Finding inefficient systems is part of finding efficient ones. In some cases, you will configure your formula based on the current system, but that does not mean it is perfect. You will need to adjust your systems in an effort to make them more efficient.

Having the skills to identify the formula within a system will give you the tools you need to create or enhance systems. All systems are based on fundamental formulae. Even if they may seem complex, they are basic at their core. Learning to separate the sub-systems from the larger systems will help simplify things so that a true understanding can take place. With the deep understanding, you will be able to find all the benefits or problems within the system.

CALL TO ACTION:

Start with a simple system and identify the formula that drives it. As you go through this process, you will surprise yourself as to how simple the formula really is. All complex formulae are made of simple ones just as complex machines are made from simple ones.

NOTES:

CHAPTER 5 - BECOME A PATTERN MATCHER

You can easily see how a simple act of matching patterns and looking for consistencies can elevate you to a maven in somebody's mind.

This is not a chapter on statistics; however, the subject of statistics plays a huge role in pattern matching. Statistics relies on pattern matching. We should look at the subject of pattern matching as a much broader subject than just statistics alone. Statisticians use math formulas that go beyond simple averages. We are going to look at pattern matching from a different point of view. Statisticians see those things that are similar and measure those things. We are going to understand that patterns are affected by external forces.

I wanted to include a chapter on this subject because it is so important to search for success formulas. My expertise is not is statistics, but I have written programs to calculate statistics, and I do have an understanding of the subject. I don't want to get bogged down in a bunch of statistical theory; however, there are a number of points of value we can get from this subject. If you find this subject to be challenging, you should not feel alone. It is a subject that we must have a respect for because of the power it gives us in our plight of understanding. Just as Ivan Pavlov observed from watching his dog, even dogs learn to find patterns. In his experiments, he rang a bell when he fed his dog, and the dog learned the pattern. Each time he rang the bell, the dog began to salivate. It would be similar to the way your own dog may get excited at the sound of the can opener or when you grab the leash. Those are things the dog would not naturally associate with an activity, but the dog learns that matching patterns is part of life.

How to establish a pattern

In order to establish a pattern, we need to understand that two points create a line—a truth straight from our elementary school math class. In pattern matching, three points make a pattern. When we find those three consistencies, we know we have the beginning of a pattern. Patterns, like systems, exist all around us. There are obvious patterns and patterns that are not so obvious. We become biased by some patterns because of the historic reliability of those patterns. The way we will approach finding patterns is by using a series of tests. These tests include what I call "markers." A "marker" is a test of a future point in the pattern. Each time we hit a marker, it strengthens our pattern. Markers are not complicated. In fact, they can be relatively simple in nature. Pavlov's dog had established a marker. His marker was the ringing of the bell, and the feeding was the hitting of the marker. Once his dog established that a pattern existed and consistently hit the marker, the pattern was reinforced.

At this point, you may be asking yourself, "What is the difference between finding the system and matching the pattern?" The difference is that pattern matching is the skill one uses to find the system. I started with systems because they are an easier concept to understand, but the skill you will hone is one of matching of patterns. The skill of matching patterns has its own system. Like statisticians that use math formulas, control groups, charts and other tools, we are going to base our system on some tools, as well.

Consistency is the core of patterns

Consistency is at the core of matching patterns. Likewise, inconsistency is just as valuable. An inconsistency is just as important as finding the consistency. Why? An out- of-pattern event will signal a possible change in the pattern. We are not just looking for inconsistencies to find a pattern change, but we are looking at inconsistencies as a pattern of their own. This skill will be one that you will practice every day of your life. We learn to spot those things that are purposefully designed to mislead us. As we perfect this skill, we understand that certain behaviors are to be expected. If we see a behavior that is inconsistent with what is expected, we look for the reason.

The truth is that we have biases that always get in the way. We have to learn to overcome those biases if we are to be good at the craft of pattern matching. How we establish our markers will tell us if we are seeing a pattern consistency or just a biased view of the pattern. In order to protect ourselves from biases that may influence our observation, we should try to gather information for multiple unrelated sources. We have seen how public opinion has been influenced by biases from mass marketing ad campaigns to news reports and political parties. We should avoid seeking only those markers that only support our bias.

The most important point we should all learn and understand about patterns is that there is always a consistent pattern. The pattern may not last for very long, and when that pattern ends, another one begins. Patterns can be stacked. That is to say, that when there are inconsistent patterns, there is an underlying larger pattern that is consistent. If you are observing what appears to be an erratic pattern, look for the larger pattern. Likewise, the core pattern is always a consistent pattern. <u>If we observe a group of patterns that are inconsistent with a singular consistent pattern, the consistent pattern is the core pattern</u>.

Patterns can be interpreted.

Stock traders use a charting program to look for patterns; they use some technical indicators to help identify key changes in the pattern. Highly skilled technicians have honed the skill of interpreting the indicators and may have developed some of their own along the way. Most of the technical indicators are based on the moving averages. There are exponential moving averages; there are simple moving averages. Watching how a ten day, twenty day or fifty day moving average moves relative to the others is an indicator in itself. A good technician will use multiple indicators to reinforce the pattern. If there is multiple agreement among the indicators, then that serves as its own pattern. An indicator that disagrees with the pattern may not indicate a problem with the pattern. More disagreement than agreement will force the trader to wait for agreement among the indicators. By watching other market activity, the trader can then determine if this pattern is a consistent pattern of its own or if it is being influenced by the larger market patterns. If you want to be a stock trader, find some books or seminars and study the technical indicators. For a head start, you can apply the skills you learn here.

What are the markers we look for?

A medical doctor will observe symptoms in a patient. These symptoms are markers for the pattern. There are some symptoms which are stronger than others. Doctors must fight against biases to determine what ails their patient. If there are symptoms that must exist to support their belief, then they try to find out if the patient is displaying those symptoms. A person who tries to identify whether a person is telling the truth is also a pattern matcher. This is done by recognizing patterns based on consistency. This is a very important part of pattern matching. You have to learn how to identify consistency. I have found through my exploits that this is one of the hardest things for people to do.

Let's say you are a military strategist, and you are watching your enemy. You gather intelligence in an effort to see what they are planning. Nothing happens in a vacuum. This means that watching an enemy's movement of assets can be interpreted as a certain type of plan. A military strategist would ask the question, "Is the enemy planning an assault or an act of aggression? What assets or activities would have to be in place?" If the strategist sees those things happening, and it is consistent with his theory, then it is easy to find the pattern. In other words, the strategist would establish markers. These markers would be something as simple as triage units on the move. That would indicate some sort of plan for casualties. If that marker is not hit, then it is nothing more than an exercise.

The U.S. military planners are masters at pattern matching. They have created a science around it. There are things that are considered "Classified" that, on the face, may seem benign, but if you are an enemy state and you learned of these things, you may put together the pattern. This is why military planners strive to keep some simple activities hidden from view.

Applying patterns

During WWII, the Allied forces carried out a number of misdirection activities designed to fool the Nazi regime into committing forces where they would be ineffective. For example, the Germans knew that eventually the Allied forces would mount an invasion. It would have been pointless for the Allies to try to convince them otherwise. So, instead of behaving as though they weren't or trying to hide it, they decided to create a fake invasion force. This did two things: it forced the Germans to commit troops in areas where there would be no invasion, spreading their already thin resources even thinner, and it gave the Allies cover to carry out missions that the Germans would have discovered anyway. So, what they did is create a pattern that would be consistent with an invasion force. The inconsistent activities, those associated with the real invasion force, had to be executed in secret. As long as consistency with the pattern could be maintained, our military could sell the fake invasion. There were numerous covert tricks that were designed to keep the Germans at least having to respect the possibility that the fake invasion force was real. In fact, on D-Day the rouse was so successful that Hitler himself would not allow the troops guarding against fake invasion to move because he so believed that the real invasion was going to occur where the fake invasion forces were. This is because the Allies created a pattern and kept it consistent up to the time so that an inconsistency would not matter. And even then, a bias made it hard to accept.

Consistency of inconsistency

I get particularly frustrated with politicians because so many of them do not realize they are being inconsistent. In fact, the next layer of a pattern matcher is to look for the consistency of inconsistency. I know this is getting confusing but when a system or process has more inconsistencies than it has consistencies, that process is so incredibly unreliable that it fails to be called a "process" or a "system" in my mind. When it becomes evident that the system is built on inconsistency, I have to conclude that the system itself is a rouse. Remember that a consistent pattern always exists. This means that consistency of inconsistency is a consistent pattern for a deliberate rouse. A trained professional with the skill of lie detection will use this tool. When detectives ask questions of suspects, they will often ask the same question a number of different ways. They will ask seemingly unrelated questions and will even take turns asking the same questions. The goal here is to establish a line of consistency. If they suspect an inconsistency, they will drill down to find out more. If they find a series of inconsistencies, they know they are dealing with someone who is being dishonest.

Only a skillful con artist can pull off multiple layers of consistency. It takes practice and lots of planning. Remember, I am not advocating using these skills for dishonest purposes. We don't want to misuse our superpowers. Pattern matching is based on consistency and inconsistency. When you get good at laying down markers and watching the pattern, you can then become adept at predicting the pattern. When you spot a pattern, you need to follow it to its next logical conclusion. This takes setting aside biases and other influences that get in the way of our logical model. We use these things in our jobs and relationships, but we rarely practice them in the larger arena of life. When we become avid practitioners of this, we begin to see life in a whole new way.

Using patterns to predict outcomes

For some people, pattern prediction is more of an instinct. Steve Jobs had a way of predicting things. His ability to see how external influences affected a pattern is legendary. He did not rely on a wider view of opinion because he relied on his instincts, not commonly studied patterns. He understood that people in the current market place seek to be entertained rather than informed. He leveraged what he saw as a pattern. Jobs recognized that instead of people becoming informed, they would rather reach for the information quickly when needed. It is odd that in today's age where information abounds, so many people are uninformed. Why be informed when information is so readily available with just a few keystrokes on a computer keyboard?

The creation of music-sharing sites such as Napster brought rampant copyright infringement issues because people would share music instead of paying for it. Jobs recognized that the public really wanted a different way to consume music, so while others were busy fighting copyright issues, he created a system around it – iTunes. He understood that music needed to be easily portable and obtainable. What he did was put together concepts that already existed into a single easy-to-use package that made it easy for people to consume the available content. Consumers had been buying CD's from the music store and converting them to the mp3 format for portability. ITunes became a platform for downloading music directly to mobile devices. With agreement from the music industry, they created a pricing model that would allow consumers to enjoy the music without a huge expense or copyright problems. The system of buying CD's and converting to mp3 formats was challenging for most consumers, so downloading illegal copies was an option many took. The new system of competitively priced music with an easy download format solved the issue for the vast majority of consumers. The system saved the music industry; however, it forever changed it. Now, almost anyone can become part of the industry.

Since this model could be repeated, the process begins to take on a life of its own. For example, iTunes allowed the iPod to happen; the iPod became the iPod Touch, which opened the interface to the iPhone, which lead the way for the iPad. What started out as a new way to consume music became a new way to consume all kinds of content. The model was based on mobile content consumption and an interface to get to the content. Jobs took a system which existed and modified it, added to it and created what we now know as the smart pad industry. Apple really didn't pay attention to market research. If it had done market research asking people if they wanted a Smart Pad, the results of the research would likely not have told you this. In fact, Smart Pads were nothing new; they had just not been introduced to the market when the market was ready to accept the idea. Timing is a critical component in the market as well as the pattern. What the market needed was to understand its purpose and up until that point, it was not clear to the market what that purpose was. As mobile broadband networks became available, the market began to find the value.

Watch for the things that influence patterns

When we look at a pattern, there are those things which influence the patterns. If a pattern remains consistent, then it is easy to predict its path; however, it is the outside influences on the pattern that are the ones we learn to pay attention to. We should analyze how the Smart Phone has impacted PC sales. It would have seemed a few years ago that the personal computer could never be displaced. The advent of the Smart Phone changed all that. Since most people only engaged the PC for a limited number of uses, (e-mail and web browsing), the Smart Phone has replaced the PC as the "go to" device, just as cell phones replaced our land-based phone lines. With the 3G and 4G networks and Smart Phone technology, information is now available "on the go." This is an outside influence that has greatly impacted the pattern of use of the PC, telephones and cameras.

Here is a story of how an alert computer attendant found a pattern that led to the problem. The computer system attendant notices that a system would hang within an hour of its memory usage starting to rise. It is common for memory usage to go up and down on a system at any given time, but for this particular system the pattern was reasonably consistent. What happened is that a process encountered a particular block of data and because the program had a memory leak, the program could no longer release the memory. The system had no choice but to keep allocating more memory until the system simply ran out of memory and hung. The outside influence was the memory leak trigger. The pattern was the normal up and down memory allocation. The alert attendant became aware of this pattern and started to notify people of the pattern of the problem. To get the computer to start responding, administrators would simply reboot the computer system. As often happens, people will see the reboot as the resolution to the problem instead of what it really was, a temporary fix. These problems do not get reported back to the developers because a small amount of downtime for the reboot is acceptable compared to the amount of time spent trying to research the issue that the pattern found. The real fix was to address the application and fix the memory leak. In this example, we should try to address the real problem instead of just addressing the symptoms. It is always better to find the problem!

Patterns are all around us

You can easily see how a simple act of matching patterns and looking for the consistencies can elevate you to maven in somebody's mind. A pattern is only good as long as it works. And it always works until it doesn't. Pay attention to patterns. They are all around us. People, animals, weather, and nature as a whole is full of patterns. We hear so little about the skill of recognizing patterns that it is overlooked by so many. Pattern recognition is the most powerful superpower a maven can possess.

In watching a work crew that has been together for

years, it becomes obvious that they have learned each others' patterns. A coach watching a game's video can pick up patterns in the other team's players. We concentrate on memorization games and strategy games, but if you want to hone your skills, seek out games that will enhance your pattern matching skills.

CALL TO ACTION:

Lay down your own markers by taking processes to their logical conclusions. When processes don't match the pattern, look for those influences that cause the pattern to adjust. You will have to practice this often, but the better you get at this skill, the better you will be at predicting outcomes. When your outcomes don't happen, find the reasons. If you see a great deal of inconsistency in your patterns, you have a process that is being manipulated by outside forces.

NOTES:

CHAPTER 6 - RELEARN HOW TO LEARN

*We are taking the attitude with our
learning that it is; not "What is the
answer we seek?", rather "Why is the
answer we seek?"*

To enrich our understanding, we have to consider that learning is a key to making this happen. One of our struggles comes from our ability to reinvent ourselves when it comes to learning. We must relearn how to learn. Learning is a natural part of life. As we get older, learning becomes more difficult. A four year old has an advantage over adults when it comes to learning how to learn. Young children are not only starting their learning process in earnest; they are also developing their skills of how to learn, which they will carry with them for the rest of their life. As we get older, we tend to focus on what we learn and less on how to learn. If you have spent time with four year olds, you notice they tend to follow each question with the question, "Why?" If we can put ourselves into that mode, we can extend our own ability to learn and understand.

We all have various talents

Some people are gifted with talents that are what we call the intangibles. These gifts come in the form of art, music, math and so on. In his 1983 book, Frames of Mind: The Theory of Multiple Intelligences, Howard Gardner introduced the now accepted theory that we have seven unique intelligences. Everyone possesses them all in varying levels. We are taking the attitude with our learning that it is; not "What is the answer we seek?", rather "Why is the answer we seek?"

I have had many people tell me that they have to see things in order to learn them while others will explain that they need to do the action to learn. Most people will go to illustrations before they read the text, but at the end of the day there are only two ways we comprehend things. It does not matter how you see yourself as a learner. We can all use the same set of tools and accomplish the same goals. It is very important that a maven has a good memory. Now, before you throw your hands up in the air and close this book, know that this IS a trait you can foster. There are many courses and books on the subject – though I will not address them in this book.

You can work on your memory skills

If you are having a problem with memory, you will need to find a way to enhance it. It is not my role here to embrace a given method because, frankly, there is no "one size fits all" for this. People will remember things based on their own personal experiences. Your health, stress levels, sleep patterns and cardiovascular fitness all play a huge role in your memory. A good memory will become valuable when discussing some particular areas.

I will be giving you some specific methods upon which you will want to concentrate. Using your memory is much like using other parts of your body. If you want to be proficient, you have to use it and practice with it. One of the things that I have done to help me remember things is to break them into chunks that are easier to remember. Conventional wisdom says a telephone number is about the length of number most people can easily memorize, but I would suggest that is a very conservative estimate. Past ten digits and it gets more difficult for people to remember because they attack the problem the hard way. Think about this: Is it really harder to remember 3 as opposed to twenty-three (23)? They are both just words, like cucumber or milk. Is cucumber harder to remember than milk or vice verse? If you take the ten digit number 214-245-2283 and break it into a 2 or 3 digit item, then you can remember 4 items vs. 10 items. If you try to remember two(2), one(1), four(4), two(2), four(4), five(5), two(2), two(2), eight(8), three(3), that is 10 items you have to memorize. Now let's look at it differently: two hundred-fourteen(214), two hundred forty-five(245), twenty-two(22), forty-five(45). That's only 4 items you have to memorize instead of 10. The last 4 numbers we can either split in two or keep them as a 4-digit block, and some are easier than others.

The same approach can be applied to memorizing Bible verses, song verses or poems. We can learn the verbiage of a simple saying or phrase. If we took on the verse as a series of phrases, all we have to do then is remember the sequence. If we take this approach and add to it a way to tie the phrases together into a cohesive thought, we can remember the verse without a lot of effort.

Working on your logic skills

Logic skills are another one of those skills you will want to hone. There are numerous board games and computer games that can help you with logic. Strategy games are particularly good, but if you want to hone this particular skill, computer programming is, by far, the best area to study to enhance your logic skills. Logic skills are hard for some people because they have become so reliant on using their memories for most of their lives of learning that they never develop the logic skills. Computers work in a world of binary, which means there is no room for guessing. Challenging yourself with computer programming works well because it forces you to work in a world of absolutes. The computer doesn't assume to know what you mean, It will only do what you tell it to do. This approach forces the logic to be correct without assumption.

If we revisit our four year old and the all the "Why's" that are asked, it is apparent in their attempt to learn there has to be a logical reason for it. A friend once observed me talking to a four year old and said to me, "You explain things too much for her." I pointed out that she is at the age where learning is her main focus. If you explain enough, she will learn all she can; however, if you only give her a little bit – what she already understands - she is not learning anything new. If she does not understand, she will keep asking questions until she does. We have to practice having a four year olds curiosity if we are going to relearn how to learn. If you want to be a maven, you must practice these skills and, like all maven skills, you will find it easier and easier the more you do these things.

Self esteem is a motivator to learn

Your self-esteem will help drive you. Failures are a part of success. Failures teach us where we need work; success is only the fruits of our efforts. There is no measure of books to read that will replace the act of practicing the skill. One of the attitudes I have taken when it comes to doing something new to me is, "Don't let it beat you!" You have to take the attitude that you are going to win – it will not beat you. Every time you allow a process to make you give up and walk away, you have allowed it to beat you. Don't let it. When I'm working on things with my friends and I give them tasks I want them to learn, I will not allow them to quit. It is too easy to simply quit the task. I would not give it to them unless I was certain they could do it. In cases where frustration is beginning to get the best of them, I will simply say to them, "Don't you let that _____ beat you!" If you are keeping score, here is a rule you need to take to heart: Failures are part of it; success is the only outcome; do not let it beat you.

Learn as though you are going to teach

As you take on a new subject, remember to gain understanding by taking the attitude that you should be able to teach someone else the material. If your attitude toward learning is that you will be teaching someone else the material, you will automatically try to understand it in a way that you will be forced to articulate it with some skill to someone else. I have always visualized myself as a teacher. When the material is new to me, I consider what I would have to know about it to explain it to a group of students. This approach has been of great benefit to me in making sure I could overcome questions others may ask about it. I may believe I understand the material, but if I formulate questions others may have, I will attempt to answer those questions in my own mind. This gives me the ability to understand the material.

Rote vs. Rule

There are two basic ways we learn: Rule learning and rote learning. Rule learning is logical understanding, working through the problem in logical steps. Rote learning is memorization, usually by repetition. You could try to memorize all the combinations of gears sizes to come up with a result or you could apply a mathematical formula and figure it out when you need it. When learning facts such as dates, symbols, sayings, multiplication tables, chemical weights, rules, vocabulary words and so on, memorization or rote learning is required. Learning percentages, like calculating a tip, on the other hand, is rule learning.

Rule Learning
Understanding the logic and mechanics of how things work together.

Figure 2 Rule Learning

For instance a 15% on a $20.00 check is $3.00 because 10% is just moving the decimal over to get $2.00 then take ½ of that and add remainder.

Rote learning is a necessity for everyone, and most

people tend to use this more than rule learning when either could be used. What is interesting is to go back to the 4 year olds we were talking about before. The reason they ask, "Why?" so much is that they are trying to make logical sense of what you are saying from their 4 year old perspective of the world. They are learning WHY something is and not just accepting and memorizing that it is "just the way it is."

Learning how a system works requires one to understand the logic of the system first, then memorize the components. Rule learners are generally good at math and science. They will gravitate toward mechanical skills and/or computer related activities. A technical minded person can easily adapt from one area of study to another because technical processes are generally transferable. The Wright brothers were bicycle mechanics who took an interest in aviation and built the first powered flying machine. As technicians, they used what they knew from the bicycle field and applied it to

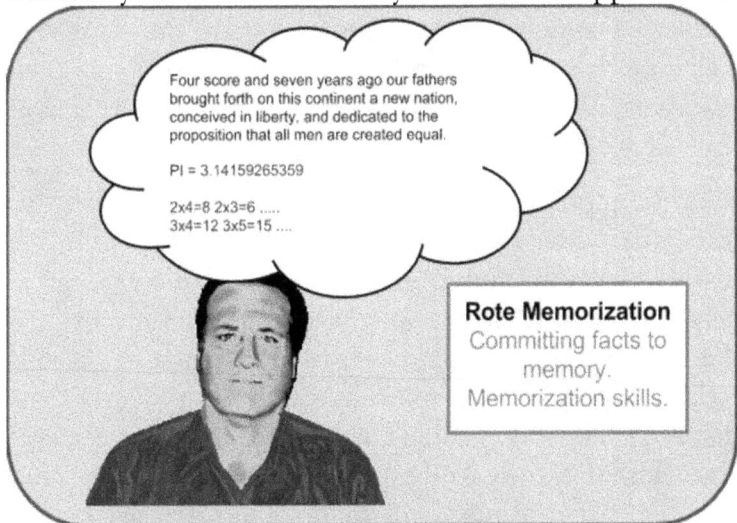

Figure 3 Rote Learning (memorization)

the aviation field. In addition, they observed birds in flight and noticed how the birds controlled their flight by using their tail feathers and changing the shape and direction of their wings. They were logically learning how the airplane would have to be constructed in order to design the Wright Flyer. It was not enough to be able to make the machine fly; it also had to be controlled, and it had to be able to land. What is amazing about these two men is that once they proved the concept, the flood gates opened up this technology in a way we have rarely seen in human history. This shows how important it is for people to learn these skills.

A rote learner is someone who will gravitate to historical information, like someone who can spout the batting averages of the players on a particular baseball team. A rote learner tries to carry everything in his or her memory with the hope of needing the information later. There are a lot of things we can and have to learn in this manner; for example, our basic math tables are generally learned through memorization, as is the alphabet. Religious leaders have relied on rote learning in their teachings. Traditions and a lot of our culture is tied to the way we rote learn.

Like the alphabet, we sometimes use songs to help us remember. Many cultures have used folk songs to pass a history down to future generations. This was a good way to do it because the song was sung over and over so the story would maintain consistency; whereas, merely repeating a story over and over can end up with a quite distorted tale. If you have ever played the game where you whisper a story to the person next to you, then they whisper it to the next and so on, then the last person tells the story out loud and you find that it is a skewed version of the story you originally told, then you know it doesn't take many repeats of the story to get it way off base.

All learning is either rote, rule or both

Some people classify themselves as being visual learners. While it is fair to say you rely on seeing something to either logically understand it or memorize it, seeing it is really only a means to an end. A maven still has to hone the skills of memorization and logical reasoning (rote and rule.) Mavens can use their memory to collect facts and even store ideas for designs. A maven can also analyze a process and logically break it down. Both of these areas are particularly important. Remember, the definition of a maven is one who understands. Sometimes, that means listening to more than the words being used. Listening to what is needed versus just what is wanted.

If you know how to learn properly and hone your skills as you go, you will get more out of school. The unfortunate part about schools is that the institution itself rarely trains people on the art of learning. Teachers simply focus on the material. Some of the traditions of teaching in schools has been passed down for generations. In recent years, schools have tried various methods, but at the end of the day, we are all individuals with various attention spans. We have different interest, different memory skills and certainly different analytical skills. I was not a particularly good student in high school. In fact, I was fortunate to have graduated. It was the skills I gained after high school that propelled me along. School was a total bore to me, so I was not concentrating, and I was also still working through some self-esteem issues related to my job situation.

Learn to teach yourself a subject

When I attended college in my adult years, things were much different. I did not learn to be a computer programmer in school. The only reason I went back to college as an adult was to get a degree to make myself "official" and because employers wanted to see it on a resume. I taught myself to program computers. At the time, I was working in a manufacturing shop as a tool and die maker. I took on computer programming as a hobby. This was in the early 1980's when personal computers were just coming on to the scene. My first computer was not even a PC; it was a z80 based computer using the CP/M OS. What's important here is that I saw the computer as a tool. Many of the early programs I wrote were to assist me in the die shop. Programming became a passion for me. By the time I took my very first computer course, I was already an accomplished programmer, with Point of Sale applications running in a production environment. My wife was a self-taught medical transcriptionist, as well, and we had a small business out of our home. There were many programming opportunities that kept me focused.

College was about getting credit for what I had already accomplished, but it was not a total waste of time. My learning skills were starting to bear fruit. My grades were outstanding. I was able to get a lot more from education than when I was back in high school. This is the point of this book. If you are a student or thinking about becoming a student, the skills this book outlines will be very helpful to you. I wish I had honed the skills earlier than when I did.

I sat and watched other students attempting to learn computer programming for the first time in the classroom and in the lab. It was apparent that there had to be a passion for the subject, as computer programming is not a subject you can master without having a drive or passion for it. I feel that we approach this subject in such a way that it turns a lot of would-be programmers away.

Learn to identify the problem, then solve it

If I needed to get to the store and walking or running was my only way to get there, running to the store would carry a different attitude than just running as exercise. In other words, the run would have a purpose outside of the exercise it would create. For new students, subjects such as computer programming, the entire lab exercise is just that. It is hard for a student to find the value in an exercise. We hear of high school students complaining about seemly irrelevant subjects. In the next chapter on transferable skills I attempt to address some of this. The real problem with education is that it fails to instill value into those things we learn through exercise. For that reason, I want you to take on the subject with the attitude that there is a problem that you are trying to solve. Every subject has a problem it is trying to solve, so when you find that problem, learn how to solve it.

When I was just getting started as a programmer working in the die shop, I saw many opportunities to use a computer program to help. Other workers and I would discuss what we would be able to use it for. There were simple problems to much more complex problems. At the time, computers were still a novelty, and their use was not clear to most small businesses. I saw the potential in them before many of my co-workers. We had one particular problem that involved material yields. The part was a segmented part that we made for the oil industry. The challenge had been that the part was an odd enough shape that it was difficult to accurately calculate the material requirements by using a hand held calculator. I knew that the computer would be able to solve the problem. What was missing was the algorithm needed. Up until this time, we relied on drawing the part out full scale to get an accurate measurement. This was very time consuming. Further, it was important to know but difficult to obtain. I had theorized with others what the value would be in solving this problem with a computer.

We did not have a computer available to us for shop use, so most of what we did was on the calculator. I had to convince the V.P. of Production that a hand held computer would give us enough capability to solve many of our problems. This computer I needed was programmable but very low powered by today's standards. He agreed to get the computer for us but as part of the agreement, I would program it on my time. This was fine with me since I was just learning, and I knew there would be a lot of trial and error. The first week I had the computer I was able to show off some of the more simple problems that I had solved, but up to that point, the V.P. seemed unexcited about the results.

Segmented Part Design

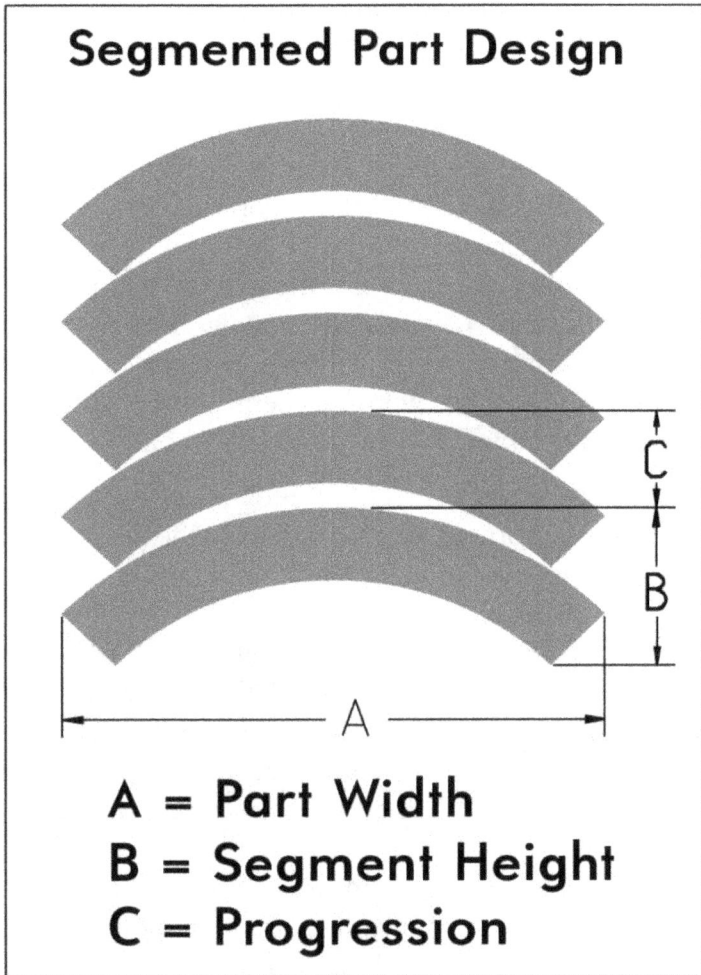

A = Part Width
B = Segment Height
C = Progression

Figure 4 Segmented Part

I knew that if I were going to make an impact with this new tool, I was going to have to solve a huge problem. The segmented part was just the ticket. I was not going to mention to him my intentions until I knew I had solved the problem.

The solution was going to require some trigonometric

functions, so I started hitting the textbooks, making sure I had all that I needed. Next, I needed some drawings showing the formulas. I spent an entire weekend drawing different configurations until I was certain I had a working model. Once I was able to see graphically how to solve the problem, I started applying the trig functions until I had a workable algorithm. It was then that I actually created the code that would run the program. It didn't take long for me to write the program since I knew how I was going to solve it. Since the material yields were part of the quoting process, the V.P. was the person who would benefit most from this calculation, although it was my team whom he relied upon for the measurements.

That Monday morning, I called him into the die shop to show him what I had done. He did not know what I was about to show him, and he was less than excited to see what new computer program I was about to present to him. I told him that I had solved the segmented part material yield problem with the computer. He sat there for a few seconds, making sure what I said was what he thought he had heard. He asked me to repeat what I had just said. He then went on to say that he simply did not believe that I had done it. In my attempt to keep from getting too far ahead of myself, I simply responded with a modest, "Well, as far as I can tell, it works." I asked him to put it to the test to validate the results, and he agreed. He spent the better part of the day checking the calculations against parts that we had previously made. He finally came back into the die shop that afternoon with computer in hand and said…"It works." I had successfully programmed the computer to calculate with accurate results what we knew to be correct from previous history. He then went on to say, "This computer is mine now. I need this more than you do." I expected this, so it was a huge confirmation for me. He did buy a second computer to replace the one he now took for himself. The computer program was able to give him an accurate segment size, length and width and subsequent progressions in seconds. It would even tell him the best segment size needed for the given material width. This was a real game changer for him. He now saw the computer as a valuable tool for the shop. This story shows that having a problem that needs to be solved can become a powerful driver for learning a subject. This also launched a whole array of opportunities for me, as I had instant credibility in the eyes of my management.

Do not accept that you have inabilities

My two sons were very young when I was honing my skills. I was able to instill into them many of the traits that I am sharing with you. When they read this book, they will know much of what I'm describing. They may not realize that a great number of people simply haven't been exposed to many of these ideas. Relearning how to learn will grant us the capability to gain valuable understanding that will lead to success in our chosen fields. Do not corner yourself by declaring your own inabilities. Worse yet, do not force yourself into a narrow definition of the way you view your own learning. We all learn in different ways, but we still have to rely on the basic rote and rule methods.

CALL TO ACTION:

When you choose the subject that you want to learn, find out what the problem is that the subject tries to solve. Learn to solve the problem. This will separate you from the rest and give you that needed credibility of being a maven.

NOTES:

CHAPTER 7 - IT'S ALL MEXICAN FOOD/TRANSFERABLE SKILLS

We can evaluate a tool for how general
purpose it is; we can do the same with
areas of study.

In our previous discussion about patterns and finding consistencies, we talked about the power of reinforcing our pattern. Knowledge about various subjects will be similar to finding these consistencies. As we learn new skills, we use the skills we learn to reinforce the knowledge we have from other subjects. A maven understands that there is transferable knowledge between disciplines. Building our knowledge base increases the skills we can transfer between subjects. It really is a simple concept, but it offers us an opportunity to leverage the things we learn.

In the first grade, we learn our alphabet, simple addition and how to count. These are the building blocks upon which most learning is based. Through the second grade we are working on these skills. It seems that somewhere around the fifth grade we start to concentrate on specific areas of study, and we forget about the reasons we learn the transferable knowledge. By the time we get to the seventh grade, we are wondering what algebra has to do with anything. As a maven, we will refocus our efforts on those things that are transferable between disciplines.

Since we understand the power of owning tools, we can also see how the simple act of owning tools will fit within the pattern of transferability to make our point. There are tools we all should have in our toolboxes are so universal in nature that we could own many of them. Tools such screwdrivers, pliers and hammers are useful to many crafts. We call them simple tools or simple machines. We can easily understand this concept, so why not apply the same principle to what we learn? We can evaluate a tool for how general purpose it is; we can do the same with areas of study.

Why is it like Mexican food?

We native Texans LOVE our Mexican food. Mexican food has various dishes made of a few core ingredients, just prepared slightly differently. I titled this chapter "It's All Mexican Food" because this is what I usually tell people who ask me how it is that I was able to learn so many different crafts. This is not meant to be derogatory to any peoples or cultures. It only illustrates a point. Enchiladas, burritos, tacos and chalupas all share many of the same ingredients-- just prepared a little differently. Enchiladas are corn tortillas with meat inside and topped with chili sauce & cheese. Burritos use flour tortillas instead with the cheese and chili sauce inside with the meat. Tacos are fried folded corn tortillas with meat, lettuce & tomatoes inside and topped with cheese. Chalupas are the same as tacos but on flat fried corn tortillas. If we take a lesson from this and apply it to our learning, we will start to see that there is a pattern there, as well.

There are skills we learn that have connections in multiple areas of study. For example, you or someone you know has the ability to learn new skills quickly. Before you simply chalk that up to you or the other person's intelligence, consider that you or the other person may have perfected the ability to transfer understanding from one area to another. One of the most important transferable skills one possesses is the skill of mastering mathematics. This skill transcends almost all areas of study and crafts. Whether you are a computer programmer, a chemist, astronomer, accountant or any type of professional, you need to have this skill. The better you are at breaking down the system and understanding how to make it work for you, the better you will be at mastering any particular new craft or subject. The ability to sell your ideas or products falls into this category, as well. It is not enough to have great ideas; you have to be able to sell those ideas. If you are in a workplace where you create tools or products within that workplace, you must have the ability to get buy-in from others. For that reason, selling is a transferable skill.

Is culinary and carpentry transferable?

Do you know there is a relationship between carpentry and culinary skills? Tape measures are incremented in inches. Most people can think in tenths easily enough because it is easy to move a decimal point, but when we are talking about measuring tapes, they are broken down in halves until they hit sixteenths and sometimes thirty-seconds. What this means is, if you are a carpenter, you see the world in sixteenths of an inch. Ironically, mechanics' sockets and wrenches are also measured in sixteenths and thirty-seconds. Why is this related to cooking? When we learn to measure, we learn about the units of measure. Units of measure follow a system of their own. Understanding this system and learning how the various disciplines use them will aid in our overall understanding.

A measuring cup used in cooking follows a measuring system similar to a tape measure used in carpentry. A pint of water weighs 1 lb., which makes a cup weigh 0.5 lbs. There are 8 fluid ounces in a cup, so there are 16 fluid ounces in a pint. Since a pint of water weighs 1.0 lb., 1 fluid ounce of water weighs 1 dry ounce. So the relationship is established at the weight of water. A gallon of water weighs approximately 8 lbs. depending on temperature. Just as a measuring tape breaks inches into halves, so do the measuring cups. This means that if you can master the ability to deal with fractions through halves, you can easily adapt from carpentry into cooking with respect to measuring.

The power of half

Here's where this is important. The ability to use the power of half is the secret to this. I can learn to half simply by doubling the denominator. For many, fractions are challenging when they should not be. Fractions are simply a way of illustrating a value, and they have a system that can be mastered easily. Since fractions are simply a way of illustrating a value, they can be dealt with as a unit of measure like any other. One of the first rules we learn in physics is to make all our units the same. This means if we are working with feet vs. inches, we convert feet to inches in order to do the math.

The same is true with fractions. Of all the math skills related to fractions we find the ability to find $1=1/1$, so we cut it in half by doubling the denominator to make it ½ or 0.5. As we cut it in half again, we double the denominator again. It is as though we multiplied the number times 0.5.

So ½ becomes ¼ or 0.5 x 0.5 to give us 0.25. All we did was use the power of half by doubling the denominator of the fraction. Most measuring cups will go down to ¼ cup, as most tapes go to 1/16ths and sometimes 1/32nds. This is incredibly easy stuff because this is a rule-learning exercise. If you are using a calculator and you need to convert these to decimals for some reason, remember that a fraction is only an unresolved division problem! There is no magic formula for converting a fraction to a decimal; the fraction IS the formula. It is that simple.

Since a tablespoon is 1/16 of a cup, we can use this method to double recipes as well. For example, we have a recipe that calls for 2 tablespoons of butter, but we want to double the recipe. We can do so by saying 2/16 = 1/8 cup. Since we are doubling the recipe, we now take the 8 and divide that in half to give us ¼ cup. This allows us to convert our measurements to cups easily. If it sounds complicated, it really isn't. Once you learn the system, you can easily work through it to memorize the pattern. The process of reducing a fraction by half requires doubling the denominator. This plays into the power of 2.

The power of two

If you are studying computers, you will eventually face this again. Since computers work off the binary numbering system, the power of 2 becomes very important. When you are looking at computer specs, you will notice things like 1024K and other numbers like 2048M. The reason these numbers may seem odd has to do with the way they are arrived. If I start with the number 2 and begin to count by doubling it each time, we will find that 1024 occurs, not 1000. As (2, 4, 8, 16, 32, 64, 128, 256, 512, 1024) shows us, we have a doubling effect with each iteration. This powerful tool will show up often in many fields and it is incumbent for mavens to learn and understand this power.

I found a textbook once on finding the patterns in numbers so that there is always an easy way to do math problems. This was fun to read through, but it also taught me a skill of doing math in my head. Really, for the most part, math is not that hard, but some people never practice it enough to get really good at it. I can look at a fraction and convert it to decimal. I can also cut a value in half or double or triple it.

If I have a recipe that calls for 3 tablespoons and I need to double the recipe, the "no-brainer" way is to measure out 6 tablespoons, but converting them to cups is probably best. Remember, 1 tablespoon is 1/16 cup, so 3 tablespoons is 3/16 cup, and I need double that. I take half of the 16, which is 8 so 3/8 cup is double the 3 tablespoons. Again if it sounds complicated, once you learn the system you can easily work through it to memorize the pattern.

If I need to find the center of a board and the board is 12 3/4 inches long, I reverse what I did above (for the fraction part, not the whole inches.) I take half of the 12 inches which is 6 inches, then for the 3/4, double the 4 to an 8 and you have 3/8. So half of 12 3/4 inches long is 6 3/8 inches long. If you want to be a machinist, you will need to learn this decimal and fractional conversion out of simple necessity.

Drill bits are sold in fractional, number and letter sizes.

Often, you will need to convert the drill bit needed to what you actually have on hand. For instance, if you need a #7 drill bit but only have fractional bits, you'll go to a chart to see what the decimal equivalent is for the #7, then use that decimal to find the closest fractional bit.

There is a relationship between skill sets and general skills. Converting from decimal to fraction, inches to metric, tablespoons to cups and so on has become a part of the way you do things. This skill of conversion will make you a standout in an area of expertise.

Creative skills are transferable as well

If you want to be a craftsman such as a carpenter or an electrician, you will want to work on your creative skills as well as your math and logic skills. What exercises would you work with to do this? You can learn drafting by taking a course, reading a book or getting some CAD software. Drawing and designing are the best exercises I have found to stimulate your creative and designing skills. These skills force you to work through those things you cannot imagine until you see them on paper. Designing a house, for example, teaches you to consider things like bathroom locations, closet locations, even where water heaters may sit. In other words, there are so many considerations when dreaming up a design that you may have to see it on paper to realize what pieces will fit best in which places. Designing a simple machine teaches us how mechanically things must work, the physics required to make it work properly and the sizing and even assembly lead us to expanding our imagination and creative skills. Eventually, as you become more skillful, you will be able to do a lot of it in your head.

These skills are very transferable. You don't have to be an engineer or an architect to benefit from these exercises. If we could take ourselves back to the second grade and understand what we were being taught, we would see that our concentration was on the transferable knowledge: math, language structure, reading and so forth. These subjects laid the ground work for our later education. However, transferable knowledge is a wide open area. There are things that are transferable that go beyond the general subjects. As a maven, we are vigilantly looking for knowledge that we can transfer between skills. When we hone the skill of pattern matching, we begin to see the wide variety of transferable knowledge that exists out there.

If you want to explore the crafts that fall into the arts, such as culinary or graphic design, you begin to see how useful this is. We talk about ethnic food menus having similar ingredients, but the real transfer happens in the methods of preparation. If you learn to cook Mexican food, you can transfer the techniques to Italian and so forth. Good cooks do not limit themselves to a single genre of food. This is true in technical fields, as well. Good technicians can move from one platform to another by using the transferable skills that they have mastered.

In this chapter, we talked about the transferability of knowledge from one area of study to the next. I wanted to introduce this concept so that you can discover them for yourself. One of the most important by-products of this is what it does for your self-esteem. With the skill of finding transferable knowledge, your confidence will increase. As you become skillful at finding and exploring transferable skills, you will become fearless in your pursuit of understanding. You will become more successful, you will be empowered. You are on your way to unleashing your own superpowers.

This is very important, and as soon as you begin to practice this concept, you will start to discover more and more applications of this concept. I could compose numerous more examples here in this book, but it is not my intention for you to use this as an introduction to the concept. I am a person who believes strongly in rule learning. If I gave you too many examples and you are a rote learner, this is where your learning would stop. It is incumbent on you to find those transferable skills that impact your life.

CALL TO ACTION:

I want to see you as a practicing member of the rule learning community, so go out there and find some transferable knowledge. It is a really fun exercise with endless possibilities.

NOTES:
_____

Think about the technologies we use today. Image how they were derived.

Can you find skills that you posses that have common skills to other things you have learned?

When faced with learning something new, do you find yourself trying to associate it with something you already know about?

CHAPTER 8 - PEELING BACK THE ONION/UNDERSTANDING LAYERS

Layers are a very powerful way to break complicated things into simpler pieces so that they can be easily understood and implemented.

On our path to success, we must visit this next challenge. This challenge to understanding is based on a construct. I have not found other books or papers on this particular subject. That is why I am introducing this construct at this time. This layering construct appears in all complex systems, so it is important to get a good understanding of it, how it works, why it exists, and how to use it correctly. Since our goal is to understand a success system, we are compelled to not only find constructs, but also to learn how to use them to our advantage.

Some words to understand

Before we get started, I need to introduce a couple of terms to ensure that we have a proper definition as it applies to the layers discussion. Our first term is "independence." The word "independence" means a process has independence from another process when it can do what it does alone. This leads us to the next term - "autonomy." The word "autonomy" is similar to "independence" in that it is an object that stands on its own. An object has autonomy when it can do what it does without the aid of another object. The next term is "common interface," which is a method, device or standard by which one layer can act on other layers.

Layers are both physical and functional

So, when we talk about layers, we are not looking at them as just physical objects or even just processes. We are looking at the layers based on items which share functionality. This means that layers can contain objects and processes. Therefore, for our purposes, it is easier if we can refer to these layers as virtual layers containing both objects and processes. We use layers for the separation they give us. We call this independence, and each layer becomes autonomous.

Layers are a very powerful way to break complicated things into simpler pieces so that they can be easily understood and even implemented. Once you begin to master the skill of pattern-matching and systems-finding, you will soon realize that most systems work on a process of layers. The skill we are talking about here is not just identifying layered systems, but of the leveraging of layers to create our own systems. This learning step is where we use our rule-learning skills. I bring this up not just because it makes learning systems easier, but it also lays the foundation that you will use to attack complicated tasks.

Layers offer problem isolation

The concept of using layers gives us a benefit in troubleshooting problems, as well. A doctor analyzes a patient's symptoms. This represents a layer. By asking questions of the patient, the doctor can find out if other issues are present without the patient being aware of the relationship. Likewise, a doctor may run diagnostic tests. In this manner, the doctor can peel back the layers to identify where the problem truly exists. This is the difference between treating the symptoms and treating the problems. Another common example is when an automobile mechanic uses the same process for troubleshooting problems. You can now see that we are not just identifying systems-- we are also learning the art of troubleshooting.

Layers in manufacturing processes

Imagine we're on a production line of cars in a factory. One plant produces engines, while another plant produces suspension parts, and another produces body parts, and so on. In this model, we have a layered approach because the engine plant has independence from the assembly plant. The assembly plant requires the engines, but the engines are built with autonomy. If the assembly plant production line stops, it has no short term effect on the engine plant, and so on. Engines can be built by the engine plant at their own speed on their own schedule, independent of the assembly. This also allows a single engine plant to service more than one assembly plant. So the relationship is not necessarily a one-to-one relationship as it would be if all the processes were under a single plant on a single assembly line. Along with this analogy we see how beneficial it is to have a common engine platform for multiple types of vehicles.

In addition to an automobile assembly operation, computers probably give us the best examples of layered systems. Computers are part of a very complex technology. If you want to develop an understanding of computers, you will want to learn how the various layers work and interact. If your desire is to program, build, troubleshoot or just use computers, you will want to learn these layers. Most people do not know that computer systems have several different layers, but it did not start out that way.

Layers evolve over time

Early computer systems were not layered, or, at least, not well layered. Early computer scientists understood the value of layers. As with all new technologies finding the layers requires an evolutionary process. The limitations of the technology change over time; therefore, the layers develop as the technology begins to mature. When the first programmable computers were built, we did not have user interfaces or operating systems. The computer was a large machine where the program and data were fed into it as it was processed. The data processing systems were very expensive spreadsheets. The software was very specific to the hardware, so portability was an issue. When the smaller computers came along, they were dedicated to specific tasks such as data entry, word processing and computer aided drafting.

Due to the limitations and upgrade issues, a separation of the hardware and software needed to exist. Thus, the hardware and software became separate layers and "Operating Systems" were created. The evolution of computing continued with many other separations, and now we have many layers: hardware, firmware, the OS, application, networking, middle-ware, data, database management, hardware drivers, virtual machines, etc. and they keep growing.

Layers form a hierarchy

In order to gain independence between these layers, we have to have a hierarchy or a "one" to "many" relationship between layers. If a process or object contained within a single layer has a one to one relationship, we consider that part of the same layer. This relationship affords us the ability to accomplish multiple tasks with a single solution. We can run multiple applications on the same operating system and even multiple operating systems on the same hardware using virtualization. Each time we encounter a process that has multiple users (other processes), we can start to see it as a layer. Once multiple processes share a "common interface" that is a layer definition.

The next logical approach is to begin to nest the layers. This means that you can have smaller layers contained with a layer (like the networking layers mentioned above.) I know if you are new to this concept, the whole thing becomes a bit mind boggling, but remember, we use the layers to simplify a complex process. In this illustration, I take on the layers that make up today's computer systems. This applies to personal computers as well as the larger mid-range systems. As systems mature, new layers are added for the reasons I pointed out earlier.

An example of that is virtualization, which belongs between the hardware layer and the OS layer.

My goal is not to teach about the computers, but to identify the layers that comprise them. As we look at the illustration, we see that the application layers are independent of the network protocols. This independence allows all the applications to have access and a common method to interact with the "network protocols." This method of layering gives application independence from having to maintain its own connections. Since the network layer maintains connectivity independently, multiple applications can now utilize the network layer. The same can be said of the "system calls" as well as the "device drivers." A properly layered system will have a common interface or method of interacting with the adjacent layers.

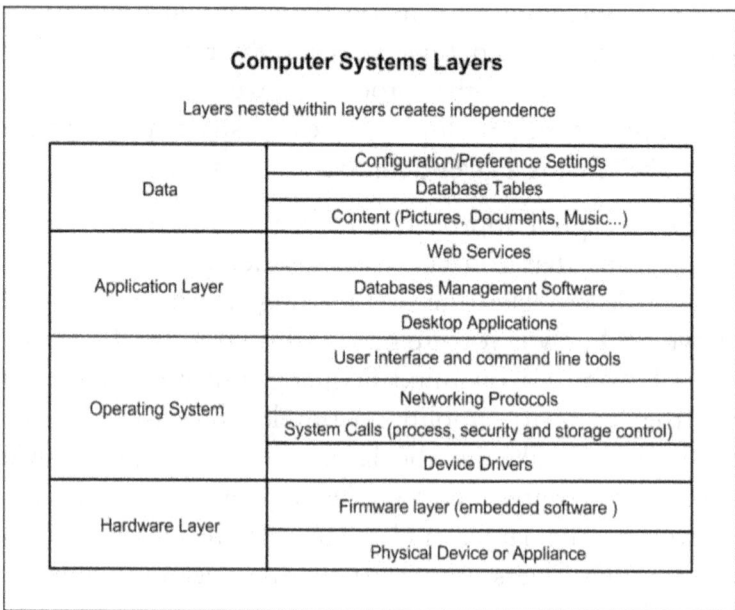

Computer Systems Layers

Layers nested within layers creates independence

Data	Configuration/Preference Settings
	Database Tables
	Content (Pictures, Documents, Music...)
Application Layer	Web Services
	Databases Management Software
	Desktop Applications
Operating System	User Interface and command line tools
	Networking Protocols
	System Calls (process, security and storage control)
	Device Drivers
Hardware Layer	Firmware layer (embedded software)
	Physical Device or Appliance

Figure 5 Layers found in computers

We will soon discuss how to refine your layered system. Often, we tend to focus on the entirety of the process and lose sight of the layers that built it. Mastering this observation will take some practice. As with all the skills a maven must learn, practice is important. Once you become accustomed to this, you will begin to see the layers where you never expected to see them.

Recognizing layers

You are already familiar with layers, but likely don't recognize them as such. Take for instance, your TV entertainment system, which consists of multiple layers. Here are some of the components that are separate layers: The TV/monitor/display is a layer. The DVD/game console/cable box is another layer. As we begin to understand layers, we find that they must have a common interface, which is nothing more than an agreed upon method by which all processes interact with the other adjacent layers. A common interface in the above example would be a video signal and audio signal. Another way of approaching this would be to consider the signal from the cable provider would be the common interface for that layer. The layer just above the set-top or cable box would have a common interface such as HDMI, Audio-Video and VGA. If this doesn't sound common, the reason is most TV's today will accept multiple signal formats or common interfaces. We cannot connect the cable signal directly into the TV unless the TV has a component for that layer built in.

So, just because our TV has an input for antenna or cable and an input for HDMI, this does not mean that the two are on the same layer. If I'm solving a problem within a system, I will seek the layer that is having the problem. I would look at each layer, starting with the common interface to diagnose each of the problems through the layers of the one containing the problem. We don't just rely on layers for designing systems; we rely on them for problem resolution, as well. By having a well designed system where the layers are properly created, we can identify problems by eliminating those layers without problems. We can easily identify the layer that is having the problem by testing the layer above and the layer below. This isolation or independence works well as a tool. We can use the process of elimination to remove layers that appear to work. So, the byproduct of our search is being able to recognize the layers, and identifying them will prevent us from looking for problems where they don't exist.

Layers make systems efficient

Systems that are not well designed with the properly used and number of layers will create a system that is inefficient. This means that just because a layer exists, that does not mean it is properly being used. Too many layers will create unnecessary complexity. Each layer boundary can be modified to have a common interface. If we look at the computer layer model, we see layers within layers. This construct is perfectly acceptable, and, in fact, it is unavoidable. In this case, nested layers have a common interface between the sub-layers and a different interface for the outer layers.

Another way to identify a layer would be based on this concept of dependence. We talk about autonomy and independence. A properly designed system has layers that have a natural independence or autonomy. Properly layered designs have dependence in only one direction. This design forces lower layers to be independent but the upper layers depend on the lower layers. Think of a building. The top floors depend on the lower floors but the lower floors do not depend on the upper floors.

In the car manufacturing example, the engine plant is not dependent on the assembly plant, but the assembly plant is dependent on the engine plant. Since the engines arrive assembled, they are placed in the frames. The other components share the same relationship. This is a common interface. The assemblies arrive at the assembly plant ready to install. This model creates simplicity and becomes a more efficient process. It also promotes the ability to scale. Each layer can scale based on its own independence. If we find there are layers that straddle larger layer boundaries in an attempt to make a single layer, this design has either too few layers or it can create a cascading effect that will create more unnecessary layers and add inefficiency to the system. This would be a layer not using a common interface rather, it has multiple. These systems do not scale well. An autonomous layer means that its reliance on the other layers is limited to the lower layer using a common interface. If an entity in a different layer has a failure, that should not affect the other layers beneath it. If you do not understood this concept, then let's look at the entertainment system as an example.

If you are not getting a picture on your TV, that may be the result of not getting a good signal, so we change signals to see if the problem persists. If the problem persists, then we know the layer with the problem is most likely the TV itself. If we get a picture with a different signal, the problem is with the signal origination layer. Each lower layer should have independence. This is where we build the relationship between functionality. The relationship is based on the concept that multiple processes can be dependent upon a single layer. The single layer or lower layer is the one with independence. Layer independence gives it the ability to scale independent of other layers. Too few layers will create complexity within the layer. We add layers as we identify the relationships. We accomplish this by looking at each process and its relationship to other processes. Then we identify a common interface. If a single process requires another single process, we say it has dependence on that process. If a process can exist autonomously and serve multiple entities through a common interface, we say that process has independence. If we find that a natural independence exists within a layer, that layer becomes a sub-layer and is nested within the larger layer. When I look at a system that is believed to be inefficient, the first place I look is the layers, I look for properly constructed layers based on independence, relationships and common interfaces. Most systems can be more efficient when layers are correctly designed.

Be open minded about layer construction.

Many times our biases get in the way of understanding where these layers are, so we have to be open to understanding the layers thoroughly. To do that, we want to start asking the right kind of questions. Looking back at the computer layer model, we can see where there is justification for certain layers. Some applications were designed where the database management was done with the code of the application. As the need for more distributed systems begin to emerge, it became evident that the database management had to be performed on its own layer. This was a major change to the system, but it allowed multiple applications to benefit from a common database host. It drove complexity from the system at the same time it became more efficient. A host dedicated to database management allowed it to do its job without the added burdens of the user interface. It also allowed for the application to scale in ways that were not obvious before. Each of the layers has autonomy; therefore, the ability to scale independently as needed.

I mentioned in the chapter on systems that even television shows follow a formula and have a system. As a storyline within a series begins to mature, we see a layering of story lines beginning. We will see the writers introduce characters and begin telling a story that seems unrelated to the primary story line. As the season (story) progresses, there may even be multiple story lines created. The primary story line will eventually have a common interface where the story lines begin to cross or connect with one another. The entirety of the story lines builds one larger story. Leveraging layers allows each storyline to have autonomy and independence. The primary story becomes dependent on the separate story lines.

Our world uses many layers

Most mavens who have expertise in single craft understand that system, but few will put it all in the context of layers; this prevents them from moving on to other fields of study. The power in layers is almost infinite. If you are a person who understands systems and that systems leverage layers, then you will be much quicker to identify these constructs.

Our world, from the local governments to the Federal Government, is part of a layered system. Our earth uses layers, businesses use layers, our atmosphere uses layers; there are layers all around us.

I don't know if it is possible to put too much emphasis on how powerful and useful layers are. If you want to reach the level of understanding that it takes to become a maven, you will need to learn to identify those layers and use the concept to transport the information to other areas of study.

CALL TO ACTION:

Find a system that you are familiar with. Analyze the system by finding its layers. Use relationships, common interfaces, dependencies to help you find where the layers are.

NOTES:

CHAPTER 9 - HONESTY BEGINS AT HOME/INTELLECTUAL HONESTY

Emotions are a wonderful servant but a deceitful master.

To enrich our understanding and unleash our superpowers we must begin working on ourselves. We face a huge challenge when it comes to finding what fact is and what is perception. This chapter is about introspection or the act of learning to look inward. I have met many highly intelligent people in my life. Some are not quite as smart as they think themselves to be. While they are certainly smart, the problem is that they can be intellectually dishonest. This leads them to making poor judgments without considering all the facts. Let's take a look at what I mean by that.

Biases are based on emotions.

One of the biggest obstacles we have on our journey to becoming a maven is the challenge of our own personal biases. Our biases are created from a number of sources, our emotions, history, education, family, news media, books and the list goes on and on. The reason our biases can be so powerful is that they are tied to our emotions. Emotions are great; I love the fact that I have emotions. Emotions are a wonderful servant but a deceitful master. We let our emotions guide us at times when we should be using our intellect instead. The problem with mixing emotions with our analytical skills is that our emotions manifest themselves in the form of biases. Biases can stand in the way of reaching the truth about facts due to the emotion they bring. It is easy to deny certain facts when we choose not to believe in them. Life is about decisions, decisions such as losing weight, stop drinking, follow God, get a degree and so forth. Deciding what to believe is part of life. We must decide that intellectual honesty is important.

Emotions are part of who we are, but they are not based in fact. What we perceive as facts in the world around us may not be facts at all. We all look at things through our own biases that come from emotion and life experience. Intellectual dishonesty is when your biases influence your finding of "fact." Intellectual honesty is about being honest with oneself in order to find the truth. We all should strive for intellectual honesty, but for a maven, it is especially important. When we find ourselves in situations in life where we need to use good judgment, our biased view can block our logical view and cloud our judgments.

Identifying our biases

Up to this point with all the discussion about patterns, layers and systems we have been building up to this. You see, I have been building a system of explanation using a layered approach. If you are reading this book with intellectual honesty, you already know the areas in which you need to work. Being a maven is not being a person who knows everything as much as it is about understanding. You cannot reach a true understanding until you learn to be honest with yourself and begin to identify your own biases.

One of the simplest ways to approach this is by looking

at a system that does not seem to ever produce results, but our biases have convinced us that it works, or it should work. In other words, as we look at the system, all we are focused on is our bias of a working system and not on the system itself and why it does not work. We should use our pattern matching skills to ensure that there is consistency from the lowest layer to the upper layers. This means that we must have good fundamentals as a base for our system. If the upper layers are not consistent with the lower layers, we most likely have allowed a bias to cause a change in the system. This is all very philosophical. Our goal is a success system we are seeking to understand, and at the core of that is making sure we have a consistent system throughout. Our biases will prevent us from examining all the facts. This is a horrible waste of time and resources.

Programming bias

Here is an example of how bias causes problems. One of the things as a computer programmer I had to learn that just because you write a piece of code doesn't mean it has to work. I would get past the syntax of code, but there is still the logic that had to be correct. I would find myself staring at the code and scratching my head and wondering why it was not getting results I was expecting. My bias was that I believed the computer was somehow getting it wrong, but the computer ALWAYS gets it right. This happens far more often than you would think. It forced me to continue to look at the code until I could figure it out. This is probably what keeps so many people from advancing their skills in the area of programming. We have a saying in the programming world: "Read the code!" What this means is read what is actually there and not what you think is there. Eventually, you will see the problem, even after staring at it for hours, but sometimes it takes another programmer who does not have the bias, to find the error.

As a seasoned programmer, I understand that this problem of bias exists. It is more obvious in the programming world but exists in most other fields; it is just not as obvious in some. The computer is very unforgiving, and, therefore, programmers have to overcome their biases or their programs simply will not work. In other areas of study, biases can exist for years, being passed along as fact from one generation to another. Our history books are full of biases based on misguided facts. We would think that history would always get things right, but unfortunately, historians are as biased as anyone.

Biases during investigations

Consider this example: A police officer is investigating a crime scene. Police officers have a particularly difficult time due to the emotional consequences all around them. From the victim to the victims' families to the drive for public safety and all the pressures that come with that, police officers finds themselves in a situation where they are in a constant struggle with emotion vs. facts. This can create a bias that the police officer must overcome in order to get to the truth. Police officers must first evaluate the evidence in order to formulate a theory of what happened. From that point on, they are looking for the consistency in the pattern to make sure that all the evidence fits the patterns, or their theory is wrong. Using the process of elimination, they cast a wide net and then starts eliminating those things that do not fit.

In this process, a bias can cause a problem. It would be easy to be emotionally attached to a theory and cast aside the evidence that would disprove it. A thorough investigator knows how to protect against this. Recently, we have seen that the "Jack the Ripper" case was solved using DNA evidence. This is a case that was full of emotion and bias. There were numerous theories put forth, casting a wide net. There were some based on conspiracy from the time and others introduced later. Criminologists have studied this case for more than a century. With modern scientific and behavioral profiles, we get a glimpse into the past in a way we have never seen before. The FBI profilers have made a science of finding the patterns of behaviors. In the century following the "Jack the Ripper" case, we can see the facts much clearer than those closest to the case at the time. We now can eliminate the biases and emotions and concentrate on those things that are important, when at the time they did not seem important. Jack the Ripper was a garden variety psychopath. He fit very closely with the profiles we have since learned about. The DNA evidence supports this. This case is an excellent study on how we can use our maven skills of pattern matching to get to the facts.

Learn to recognize dishonesty

Honesty plays many other roles as well. When you are working with other mavens, as we explore later in the book, we begin to network, and how we participate is very important. I know a lot of smart people who are dishonest with the people around them, and this is using your superpowers for evil. There are people who have created a system and have perfected the skill of being manipulative. I think more highly of mavens than to consider these people mavens, but they exhibit many of the traits of a maven. I deplore dishonesty personally because for me it is a personal insult. Any person who is willing to lie to you does so for their own personal gain. They believe they are smarter than you because they believe you will not figure out their lie. The challenge of intellectual honesty is knowing the difference between a fact and a perceived fact. Knowing not to lie to one's self is the biggest challenge to his or her plight.

Learn the power of patience

Intellectual honesty also gives us a platform for another important trait that a maven must possess - patience. Why include patience in a chapter about honesty? The chapter is really about intellectual honesty, which is a fact based system where patience is a trait balanced with emotion. I say "balanced" because the more you stick with the facts and keep your emotions under control, the more patience you will possess. Frustration is a de-bilitating emotion. It is not the opposite of patience; it is the absence of patience. Patience comes from re-moving emotion and dealing with reality and facts and seeing the big picture.

I believe patience is a key to success, but sadly many of my friends and acquaintances lack it. We owe it to our success to have patience. Failure is a part of success, and once you really believe that, it will help you develop patience. My realization came from my early days as a self-taught programmer. Early successes can drive your interests but failures which lead to frustration could stop you from advancing your craft. When you feel frustration starting to take root, it will be helpful to find another set of eyes to remove the biases.

Biases can lead to frustration when things do not work as expected, just as it did when my bias was telling me the computer was doing something wrong. Knowing that the computer was really the decider on what works and what does not work, it forced me to ensure that what I was giving it was correct. Facing the reality of logic and reasoning allowed me to have the patience to find the problem.

You see, there is a link that exists between having patience and intellectual honesty. Patience is an important trait to have as a maven and is critical to success. If you are someone who suffers from a lack of patience or you feel that you have too short of a fuse, it can be very debilitating to learning a new craft or advancing an existing one and will stand in the way of your overall success.

In this story we have 2 mechanics, they are both experienced and both have a trait of following patterns. An apprentice approaches each of the mechanics and asks a simple question. Are the bolts that fit the bell housing metric or SAE? In this story, we have an outside influence that changes the facts. The manufacturer of the engine had moved from SAE to metric. The first mechanic told the apprentice that he believed that the bolts were SAE. He had observed the pattern over history and created a bias based on those facts. The second mechanic asked the question, "Are all the other bolts on the engine block metric or SAE?" The apprentice replied with "Metric." The second mechanic said, "Then the bell housing bolts are metric as well." He too had observed a pattern and that was that the manufacturer would not make some bolts SAE and others metric on the same physical block. The manufacturer would be consistent in that pattern. The second mechanic would not allow the bias of the history to influence what he perceived to be fact. The apprentice tried both types and found that the second mechanic was right. The apprentice then learned a valuable lesson that would serve him for future use.

This is one of the life lessons that can serve us in all areas of our life. We can make poor judgments if we allow an incorrect observation of the facts to cloud our judgment-- such things as our purchases and including our relationships are impacted by this. It is said that all purchases are emotional decisions. We create within ourselves a view or bias of value. Decisions such as, what we wear, what we drive, where we live, whom we respect, or even what our favorite color is are based on emotions. As a maven, we owe it to ourselves to make sure that the facts are complete and unbiased. As we continue to enrich our understanding, we become wiser as a result of this.

CALL TO ACTION:

Try to recall major purchases you have been involved in. Think about how you rationalized those purchases. If you are intellectually honest with yourself, you will be able to identify how you arrived at those decisions. Recount how you sought the approval of others to help reinforce your decision. Use this exercise each time you are faced with a decision. You will begin to see how you allow emotion to drive decisions.

CHAPTER 10 - IT'S ALL GEEK TO ME/LEARN THE LANGUAGE

For the people who understand the
language, communication becomes
unambiguous and efficient.

You may feel that you struggle in the area of learning a new subject, that it will be difficult, or with all this talk about becoming an expert or maven, it is probably more than you can handle. You may understand that success requires a level of understanding, but you may not know how to make it happen. Our overall success relies on the success we have in learning to understand. As discussed in the chapter on systems, there is a formula for learning a subject. The next few chapters will address the system of learning a new subject. This system is the same system one would use when trying to become an expert in his or her chosen profession. My goal with the next few chapters is to give you the understanding of how some are able to easily become experts.

The importance of geek speak

In any area of study or in any field, we recognize that the people in that field speak a language of their own, or so it seems. If you don't want to get lost in a conversation with them, you need to know their language. Maybe you have read an article or a magazine advertisement, realizing you have no idea what you read or why you needed to know it. It is likely that the article used a lot of technical terms. There are valid reasons for using these terms, and that is what we need to understand. What this is about is what you may call "Geek Speak" or techno-jargon. For that reason, our first and most important challenge to becoming a maven in a chosen field is to learn the language.

Every area of study benefits by having its own language. It doesn't matter if we are talking about agriculture, computers, medicine, telecommunications, culinary, sales, publishing or automobile mechanics--each one of these industries benefit from having its language. For the people who understand the language, communication becomes unambiguous and efficient. A pair of doctors talking about a patient's condition can make their points quickly with each other. A computer technician can communicate with his or her peers concisely. In many instances, it would be virtually impossible to communicate otherwise. Meanings of words change by a simple changing of a character or two. Examples would be: Hypo vs. Hyper,

- Hyper- means over, excessive, more than normal, The prefix derives from the Greek word hyper, meaning simply "over." Hyper-vigilance meaning excessive or extreme vigilance.

- Hypo-, means under, defective or inadequate, The prefix derives from the Greek : hypo, meaning under. Hypoallergenic specially formulated to minimize the risk of an allergic reaction.

There are numerous other examples of how this works. Learning to know the difference will also help with learning the language. Looking for these patterns in words will help your understanding of the language you are mastering.

Not just a vocabulary exercise

For many who are rushing to get through their college courses, they have taken a list of words, studied a definition enough to pass an exam, and that is all they are interested in doing. THIS IS NOT WHAT I MEAN!! When I tell you to learn the language, I don't mean just learn the words. I mean that you become fluent in that language. Remember, it's not what the answer is; it's why the answer is. Learning the language means that we want to learn the language or lexicon of each field of study that we are going to become a maven for. This goes well beyond the obvious vocabulary rote style learning we did in elementary school. Understanding is our goal, so it goes with the language of the field. It is not enough to know there is a word and what it means; we have to learn how it fits, how it is used, when it is appropriately used and when it is inappropriately used. As with any language study, this is about proper usage. In an earlier chapter, I discussed the importance of having a good memory. This is the area where a good memory will become increasingly important.

Buzzword abuse

Don't be a buzzword "abuser" - people who latch onto buzz words in an effort to try to make others feel that they know the subject matter. One of the quickest ways for me to expose an "abuser" is to listen to the way he or she uses the terms. Abusing buzzwords is a dangerous practice because this can expose you as not being an expert! You are far better off to ask questions to find out more about the words someone else is using than to attempt to misuse the word yourself.

Conversely, if you wanted to lose someone in the conversation, just start throwing big, specific words around, and you can lose them pretty quickly. There are those who purposefully use words just to trip up people or to try to prove a point. I would say as a best practice approach, unless your goal is to teach, you should keep the advanced words to a minimum around those who may not understand them completely. The goal here is the "understanding," not the "misunderstanding." No one benefits from this practice, so it is only an exercise to show off your knowledge. As a teenager working in the auto parts store, there were numerous situations where others were trying to show their own knowledge, and they would use words they had heard in an effort to sound like experts. Having been exposed to these terms myself, I knew when they were simply repeating what they had heard. Later in the chapter on tips and tricks you can use this discernment to know what is valuable and what is not.

Articulation is the key

Using words that will purposefully trip people up is a trick of the propagandist, not a maven. Language and vocabulary are also part of a system, which means they have patterns and layers. The most articulate people are the ones who can understand the origin of terms and why they are used. Today, we have an enormous amount of words that make up modern languages. In this global economy other languages borrow from

English, and English borrows from other languages. It is what turns into our daily vocabulary or lexicon. In fact, the word "maven" is not known to many people, yet it has been part of our language for a long time. Understanding the history of many of these words will give us big payoffs in the process of learning the language.

Technology has aided a lot in the area of language. Imagine trying to explain what an airplane, an automobile or a computer is to someone from the medieval days. We have words that are conjoined to form new words. Some words that started out as nouns are now used as verbs like the word "text." These are all part of learning the language of a given profession. Taking this exercise on as merely a vocabulary goal, you miss most of the benefit of learning the language of the profession; that is why I am saying to learn the language, not just the words.

Real world examples

Here's an illustration: In the computer world, there are different types of memory; each one has or has had a meaningful purpose, and so it goes. We have different ones for different purposes. RAM – random access memory or volatile addressable memory. If I gave you that definition but all you know about it is a definition, and that is what you memorize, now what? This information at this point is perfectly worthless. It sounds important, but without some context it has no real meaning. So it goes with so many things in the computer field. This keeps so many people on the side lines.

In our example, we want to know more about the

specific word, so we begin to drill down on it a bit. As it turns out, RAM is the only memory that is directly addressable from the processor. In the earlier days, it was referred to as "core memory." The name came from how the technology was created rather than how it was used. This is important, why? Because there are various types of memory, and with this particular type, data has to be moved to RAM before the processor can see it or use it. In other words, data has to be addressable to be used. If you are a programmer, this is important to know. If you are building a system, the amount of RAM can affect the system's performance. If you are deciding on an Operating System, you need to know its requirements. Just having the definition without context means that we do not clearly understand the language. This context is part of the motive. Find what makes each term valuable within that area of study. Understand the history of the term.

Another example would be in the automotive field. Let's say we are looking at the specs on a car and we see some strange letters put together such as "VVT." Now in a world of acronyms and hyperbole promoting brands and other such fast talk, we may let this one slip by us. But to an automobile maven, these letters have very specific meaning. This is a relatively new terminology, so for many it may not be clearly understood. The letters refer to "Variable Valve Timing" so let's break that down. Valve timing, we might understand, but the variable part is where things get confusing. The variable in this context refers to the speed of the engine. Those of us in the car world have seen for years where camshaft profiles have dictated the use of the engine for a large part. There are different cam profiles for engines that do a heavy hauling, cam profiles for performance tuning, fuel efficient cam profiles and so on. One of the aspects of the cam is the relative timing profile it has. With VVT, the computer can adjust the cam's timing profile on the fly, gaining both power and fuel economy. A simple explanation is not sufficient to make a person understand this term enough to use it as part of a discussion, but as we drill down into the word and put some context around it, now the words come to life. They have meaning and become part of our lexicon.

Language has context

It was not my intent to teach you the words or their meanings in the above examples but rather to emphasize how important the context is to the meaning. Some words have different meanings depending on the field you are talking about. In many cases, we shorten a word from a longer word such as 'cam' for camshaft in the automotive field, the word 'CAM' in manufacturing is an acronym for Computer Aided Manufacturing. So, depending on the discipline, you will want to make sure you are clear not to confuse the terms.

There are many benefits to expanding your vocabulary. This is the area where you need a good memory. We also talked about rote learning vs. rule learning. Expanding your language into a new field is NOT just a rote exercise. You will use the rule learning skill to put the context with the word in order to make it part of your language.

One question you may be asking right now is, how would one find the vocabulary for a given discipline? Books are generally a good source, as is the internet. I will generally seek out a book that calls itself a reference.

But be careful! Not all of them are the correct kind. A book that is a good reference will have a list of vocabulary words located somewhere in the middle of the book. This is done so that the book can lay open for quick searching. Reference books are not meant to be read from cover to cover; they are meant to be referred to only when a concept or word needs to be learned or clarified. Another key feature I look for in a reference book is that it has a complete index. You will rely heavily on the index. What you will discover in a good reference book is that for each definition, there are related words presented, so use the index to find these words and make sure you understand them all. Again, there is a relationship between the words and how they are used. This is all part of building the language of that discipline. You will eventually get to where you reference the book less and less, but in the early days, don't be afraid of grabbing it and just reading and absorbing as much as you can.

Use your reference books

As a computer programmer in a large organization, I was often sought out for guidance by other programmers. They would get stuck in their program and ask for my help. I was their "go to" guy on these issues. As I would walk into their cubicles, I would look for their reference books and inevitably there they sat on the shelf in pristine condition. My reference books are discolored; pages are fluffed out and generally in not a great condition from lots of usage. As I examined their pristine reference books, I would say, "Here is the problem!! This book has hardly been used."

Another hint: when you find a reference book you really

like, consider getting two copies. I cannot tell you how important it is to have the book where you are doing the work. If you are working in a field that allows you to do your work in multiple locations, you will want to make sure you have a reference book in any place where you are going to work. It does you no good to have a reference book on your home library shelf when you are in the office and you cannot get to it. However, in today's world of the ever-present internet and smart devices, we may see the end to the paper reference books for their digital brethren. However, it is still a good idea to have at least one available.

Taking notes is not understanding

Another source of learning is seminars or group meetings where experts from a given field will meet to discuss topics. This is an environment where you will hear advanced words tossed around like candy. If you find yourself in a situation where you are just beginning to learn the language and you are in a place where you can be lost quickly, your first instinct may be to start taking notes. Here as well as all of life, you cannot serve two masters. If you are trying to take notes, you are not focusing on what the speakers are trying to convey. Remember: to be a maven you must be one who understands. If you want to reach understanding, it is best to allow your skills to work for you, and this is where it is extremely important. Think about it…how many times in note-taking have you stopped writing, looked up and realized that you've missed the whole next point of what the person just said? Your dictation skills are the only ones that benefit from perpetual note-taking during a lecture. I cannot be clearer on this! You need to concentrate on the message. Oftentimes, words that are not easily understood will gain context during the lecture. You do not want to miss this opportunity to gain the understanding. If you are constantly writing at this time, you cannot focus adequately on what is being said. I can walk away from a speech without notes, but with a good understanding of the message as I apply my concentration to the speaker. This may sound counter to what you have been taught your whole life, but let's be honest; most of us have never learned the best way to learn. We simply repeat other people's habits in the hopes of learning.

If you are thinking I am talking about rote learning here, you are likely surprised that it is actually rule learning. It is not my intention to memorize the words they are saying, but my intention to allow the speaker to formulate the context in which I need to learn the material. This is where we use our pattern matching skills too. We find that languages have trends and patterns. Learning a language is a perpetual endeavor. Our language or lexicon is changing all around us every day of our lives. New technologies drive this, trends, fads and marketing hype are at the core of this. How well we adapt to and expand our lexicon will change dramatically how we perceive and how we are perceived. The benefits cannot be over stated.

CALL TO ACTION:

There are words we hear daily that we may not fully understand. Find those words and start learning them in such a way that you can explain their meaning to someone else.

CHAPTER 11 - BELIEVE ME, MY MOTIVES ARE PURE/UNDERSTANDING THE MOTIVATION

*For each discipline there is always a basis
of how and why we do what we do.*

We all have our own motives for doing things. In an earlier chapter, I discussed finding the fire in our gut, or motivation. In learning a craft, starting a business or any other pursuit in life, we are driven by numerous motives. Part of our struggle is to find within ourselves that which drives us forward in pursuit of success and understanding. In this chapter, I want to discuss how to identify the motives behind what we are trying to achieve. Self-actualization is a very powerful motive, but there are others. Your superpowers will ultimately be determined by how committed you are to success. In the pursuit of success, the power of understanding is based on your own motives for pursuing each endeavor.

The how and the why

So far, our path to understanding has taken us to empowering ourselves with options, learning systems, identifying patterns, learning the power of layers, learning the language, and dealing with our biases. Now, the next step to empowerment is understanding the motive behind a field of study. I enjoy seeing young children express curiosity at things and questioning things. The inevitable "Why?" question will emerge sooner than later during the conversation. It is an important part of understanding and one we should exploit to its fullest. Talking about the motive of a field, that is the "how and why." In our enrichment of understanding we must learn the motives behind the field.

In the previous chapter, I discussed that vocabulary is more than the language of an area of expertise. In that discussion, I concentrated on the context of the meaning more than rote memorized version. Now we will drill down even more to tie all the language pieces together by adding the context of the motive. This is not to be confused with a profit motive or a safety motive; this is the motive of how it all functions.

Realizing the system and understanding it

In every field there is logic behind the concepts. Each area of study or expertise has a formula or system upon which it operates. Understanding the mechanics of the system is the basis for motive or context. It is not enough to know what the parts of a car are called or where they fit; we need to understand what makes the engine run, the transmission shift gears, the brakes work, the electrical systems function, and so on. I use the car example because of its relevance to all of our lives, but we could easily be talking about software, computer hardware, chemistry, carpentry, culinary arts, medicine etc.

In our previous chapters, I focused on patterns and systems, layers and logic and how we apply these. This is where that will become most useful. You see, I can tell you how gears mesh together and even show you pictures and it may seem so easy, but there is more to it than that. The number of teeth on each gear has relevance to how the gear should be used. There are different types of gears: ring gears, pinion gears and worm gears. Each one has its proper use. There are many places where gears are best used. All of these discussion points about gears play into the motive - why and/or how we use them. We could easily have this discussion about other areas. For each discipline there is always a basis of how and why we do what we do. The motive – the how and why - can include the mathematical formulas used in the field, the crafts included in the field. We even get into special materials, type of materials, what certain machines are used, if certain machines are used.

Real world examples

Let's visit a furniture shop. In this furniture shop, we build desks made of hard woods and veneers. There are tools such as planers, sanders, routers and table saws, miter saws, jig saws and pin guns. So far, we are merely speaking the language, but here we want to know more about the craft. In a corner of the plant, the saws are ripping boards, while others' saws are chopping them down to size. We notice there is a setup station where a strange looking device is set up with a special router tool. It is a dove-tail cutter. What does it do? It cuts dove-tails in the end of boards. Our goal here is to learn the motive. The motive for the dove-tail is that it allows us to join the corners of the drawers to create a strong bond. This method is the strongest way to corner join two boards. We understand there is a strength motive behind doing it that way. It is certainly not the easiest way to do it and not the cheapest; this is purely for quality purposes.

We can seek out the motives in all of the different processes within the furniture shop. It takes some time to gain this information, but a maven will seek this out. Maven can find the system in these motives and transfer the knowledge they have learned from other area of expertise into this process to build a strong understanding of the way the furniture shop functions.

Let's pretend that you are a computer consultant. As a computer consultant, you know all kinds of things about computers, how they work and so on and so forth. But as a consultant, companies hire you to come into their business and perform some sort of a task. Let's say you are invited into a business where some sales people have been working for years and the system they have for data management is a set of file cabinets, lined up against the wall. There are file cabinets for all kinds of different types of paper work. The manager says to you that he or she wants to automate this and put it all on the computer. Unless you have already faced this situation, you may not know where to start.

By now, we have enough skills to be able to understand what has to happen here. We first need to know what the different types of papers are; this is the language of the business. We need to know the motive of the various types of papers. Now we can start to build our understanding of their system. We are looking for the layers in their system. Only after a complete evaluation, can we then find a solution for them. As a maven, we use transferable knowledge from other systems and processes into this one to find the best system for them. We may have to replace key parts of their system for better ones. One of the challenges you may face as a maven is that a system may be plagued with legacy motives that are hard to overcome because change is not easy for some. Change has a cost.

As you begin to drill down into the motive to understand it, you may face those words a maven does not want to hear: "That's the way we have always done it." This is very frustrating for a number of reasons. Enough time has gone by since the system was devised that nobody knows why the system was set up the way it was. There usually is a fair amount of reluctance to change a system. The users believe it is a good enough system, and they are comfortable with it. Here is an example of how motives can be misplaced within a business. The good news is that businesses are rarely autonomous. There are other businesses like them. Others have faced similar challenges within their systems. So a maven (being one who understands the bigger picture) knows that all you have to do is find the consistencies and match the system to their real needs.

Overcoming the legacy bias

Here is a story to illustrate how motives can be forgotten. In our story, we have five monkeys in a cage with a stair case. At the top of the staircase is a bunch of bananas. As the monkeys see the bananas and begin to scale the stairs to get to them, all of the monkeys are sprayed with water from a strong water hose until they relent. With each attempt of a monkey to scale the stairs, the group is sprayed, and they soon relent. Soon, all the monkeys present learn the pattern and stop trying to scale the stairs to get the bananas. If one of the monkeys attempts to scale the stairs, the others in the group will try to prevent it from doing so. Once we reach this point, we can replace one of the monkeys in the cage with a new monkey. As the new monkey to the group begins to scale the stairs, the others attempt to stop it. It will quickly learn that it should not scale the stairs. As we continue replacing another of the original monkeys with a new one, the others prevent the new one from scaling the stairs; even the previous new monkey begins to take part in stopping the newly added monkey. This learned behavior is part of a group think mentality. We will eventually replace all the original monkeys with ones who do not know why they are not allowed to scale the stairs. Still, the group prevents new monkeys from scaling the stairs. They have no knowledge of the water being sprayed. It was just accepted as, "That is the way it has to be." This behavior becomes prevalent and can cause the motives to become displaced. The original motive has been forgotten, lost, or never well understood.

Businesses that have grown from very small to mid-sized businesses, single proprietors, family businesses, or entrepreneurs can be plagued with legacy processes and motives that are not necessarily the most efficient systems. Later in the chapter on developing a success system, I discuss how to identify a success system and how to improve an existing system. Entrepreneurs who are professionals in their craft tend to focus on the things they are really proficient with or like doing. Some processes within their business lack the proper motive or incorrectly focus their motives. These motives become legacy motives and are hard to change. Therefore, part of our plight is to recognize poorly formulated motives as well as correctly formed motives. Within each layer of the business, we need to assure we have the proper motives.

As we peel back the layers in each discipline we encounter, we can examine the motives within each layer. Many times, the motives are the driving force for having each layer. Motives can have a natural independence from one another enough to justify having their own layer. The example of the computer layers drives this home once again. The networking layer's entire motive is communication between other computers over some type of connection. The network layer cares nothing about the software that will use it; nor does it care about the hardware to which it is connecting. The only motive of the network layer is to establish a reliable communication method and present that method to other layers so that they may use it. This is an obvious example of how layers contain different motives.

Layering of motives

Since we can nest the layers, if we want to build a system using a layered approach with motives independent of each other, all those layers would eventually form a single system on their own. This takes a complex problem, breaks it down into smaller pieces, thus making each one more manageable. We talked earlier about how powerful the use of layers can be, but when you put them within the context of motives, it is easy to see that one can create a fairly complex solution using a straight forward approach. Properly formulated motives within each layer prevent duplication of work. When you see there is a chance that work is being repeated, this is clearly a sign of inefficiency. There is an opportunity to see if that motive needs to be moved to a different layer or create some independence from other processes.

Don't allow all of this to confuse you. This is how mavens think, this is what gives them their "superpowers." It helps to create a flowchart or some type of illustration so that you can examine each motive and layer to identify those areas where duplications may be occurring. This may force you to look at changing some of the structures to correct problems within your system. A maven leverages the tools that are readily available to create and manage such systems.

CALL TO ACTION:

Invest some time into re-evaluating the processes within your system, and look for those areas where inefficiencies can cause you problems.

NOTES:

CHAPTER 12 - HISTORY IS PROLOGUE/LEARN THE HISTORY

The technologies of the past build the technologies of the future

Why would we want to understand history in a book about success and success systems? The reason is clear. History can teach us a lot about where we are headed. The reason why we need to know the history is this: "We know where we are, but if we want to know where we are headed, we have to learn where we've been. " It does not matter which course of study you pursue or which system you are trying to emulate, there is always a history that has led up to the current state. This concept goes beyond the history we learned in school. Schools introduce history and its relative importance, but learning a craft or system will require a much deeper understanding. Where would we be if we knew nothing about our history? As the oft repeated saying goes, "Those who do not learn from history are doomed to repeat it."

How learning history benefits us

We break history down into two different periods, prehistoric and recorded history. Prehistoric history existed prior to recorded history. Since mankind has found that history can be cyclical, meaning it can repeat previous similar events, we (mankind) have begun to record the history that we may learn from it. The value of history is immeasurable so we began to record it, from cave walls, later to the written word. The Bible, the oldest history book we have, was recorded for such a purpose. There are other writings we rely on, also. Archaeology has created a way to use physical evidence to look at a different type of recorded history. Our study of history goes beyond the facts of history. We can use our maven powers to break down our understanding of history. If we focused on only one part of history, we would not get a clear view of it. Ancient civilizations recorded some events in the form of folk lore or tradition. Some civilizations gave us concepts that have made their way into modern science. Mathematics, astronomy, metallurgy, and chemistry have all benefited from ancient cultures. We don't have to go that far back to see where we came from. An accurate account of history is just as important as the history itself. If we rely on a distorted view of history, we fail to learn the lessons it is teaching us. So, part of this discussion relies on our being honest about the facts. This accuracy relies on our ability to put away our biases and consider all of what history can teach us.

We take the lessons from history and apply them to today's environment. In the study of history we begin to see the value of transferable knowledge. The reason for this is simple; we all stand on the shoulders of those who came before us. We look at some of history's most notable mavens and see that they, too, used the method of transferable knowledge to create for us some of the most valuable technologies we have. If we want to change the world, we must have an understanding of history. This book is about what it means to be a maven, how we become a maven and how mavens use their understandings, so it goes with the study of history. We study the mavens of history, we try to emulate them, and that starts with the understanding. One of my favorite mavens of history is Sir Isaac Newton. Thomas Edison is another, but there are many others. We stand on their shoulders to reach from today and beyond.

Sir Isaac Newton gave us modern science. It was his realizing principles within the physical world that established the "scientific principle." Most people only know of his work in physics, but he was also an alchemist, which became chemistry. His "Laws of Physics" concreted with us an understanding that launched a host of scientific discoveries. Space travel and satellite technology rely on principles he established in his time. The scientific principle changed what we considered to be sorcery or magic and turned into a study that can be taught to others and learned. It changed the very way we viewed the world. We began to realize that there are truths of nature that never change. These "Laws of Nature" are the basis for most scientific studies. If you want to be an engineer, you will learn these. If you are trying to become a doctor, or even a computer scientist, the basis for all technical studies can be found in these laws of nature. Additionally, the laws of mathematics are a part of the laws of nature.

The study of history is about transferable knowledge

Discoveries in one area of expertise now can be transferred into other areas. Several examples come to mind. For instance, today's engine that powers our automobiles can trace its own history back to the steam engines. Today's agribusiness can trace its roots back to the work of George Washington Carver and the peanut. Chemistry found out what it can and cannot do, due to the characteristics of the atom. We learned that transmuting lead into gold is much more difficult and expensive that it was once thought. In almost any area of expertise, there is a history from which we can learn. Even the founding fathers of the United States crafted the Constitution from lessons of history and other government systems. To study history, sometimes we only have to go back a few decades. Space travel and modern computer technologies are only a few decades old. What used to take centuries for technologies to develop can now happen at a much faster pace. What are the driving factors behind this? As stated earlier, transferable knowledge from other technologies. New technologies develop quickly because they build upon the knowledge of the past. Today, our techniques are refined. For example, our technologies automate mundane tasks, and we share knowledge at a global rate with lightening speed. All these things are part of the growth of modern technology. When Neil Armstrong uttered those immortal words, "One small step for man, one giant leap for mankind," in a single statement, he acknowledged that he stood on the shoulders of others and that those who followed would stand on his shoulders. This is the essence of how important this becomes.

If we study the history of today's computer systems, it is hard to define when the computer was actually created and by whom. We know some of the names of the players involved, and we can even understand their contribution, but we cannot point to a single person and say that this is the person who invented the computer.

The reason for this is a study in how we take various technologies to combine and create new technologies. We can trace the early understanding of computers to Charles Babbage and Blaise Pascal and their vision of a computing machine. We can see how Jean-Baptiste Falcon utilized punched plates in the textile industry that led to the use of punched cards in early data entry systems. This technology was used in the 1890 census and proved its worth in data collection by automating the process. Herman Hollerith proved the value of tabulating machines. Once this "proof of concept" was realized, the other applications were soon realized. Plainly, the lesson of history is always that application drives development. Application is the goal; transferable technology is part of the path. All systems are created from sub-systems, and new systems are derived from parts of the past combined with transferred technologies to create new technologies. We find new technologies as older technologies either exhaust themselves or other forces cause the change. Today's capabilities could not have existed prior to the discovery or the maturation of existing technologies. Computers were originally mechanical, then electromechanical, then electronic with tubes followed by transistors. Once the transistor computer existed, we had the basis and the understanding of how computers would be made to work. These transistor-based computers gave way to integrated circuits and then the microprocessor. It was the development of the microprocessor that empowered the technology to find its way into other technologies.

Modern automobiles rely heavily on computer control systems. The control modules that modern engines use for improved performance and fuel economy could not exist until the microprocessor was developed. The technologies of the past build the technologies of the future. I enjoy this part of the process because it gives me a healthy respect for the technology.

History usually records a topic's failures as well as successes, and they both help develop improvements for the future. We tend to cling to the past, but we often forget the struggles that got us here. In many cases, new technologies come from the failures of past technologies, also. Try driving an antique automobile, and you soon realize how the current models benefit from technology.

Technology course corrections

Each time there is a course correction coming, it is the result of a single event in history. Today's information age began when Johannes Gutenberg developed the movable type printing press. At the time, he had a single goal or application, but because of the impact of that one event, history and technology took a brand new path. The "One small step for man" quote comes to mind. Gutenberg borrowed concepts and added a few to create the publishing industry. More importantly, he empowered future generations by making information more affordable and available, thus leading to a more knowledgeable society. With this new availability of information, past technologies could be better leveraged into new discoveries and technologies. As in all things we do, Gutenberg borrowed concepts from other technologies to create a whole new technology.

If you are a student of economics, you want to understand how economies have functioned before. If you are a student of metallurgy, you will want to know how discoveries were made. It is all a part of the process of determining where we are headed after we see where we have been. If carpentry is your interest, you can find a deep history around that craft. Boat building was an early incarnation of carpentry. Housing and furniture making are obvious examples, but most may not realize how many tools were made from wood. In fact, the early tool makers were not machinists--they were carpenters. Today, modern machines do the work that only skilled craftsman would have been able to perform centuries ago.

It is important to learn the lessons of history. The lessons give us a respect for the craft and teach where the successes and failures exist.

We learn from our failures

Imagine if an engineer were designing a bridge and he or she did not have the benefit of past success or failures in bridge design. This would put all who used the bridge in a dangerous situation. Engineers rely heavily on knowing which designs yield the best results. If you want to become an engineer; besides the math of physics, geometry and trigonometry, you will also be a student of the history of designs. If we look at some of Michelangelo's designs, we can see he had a lot of great ideas. His designs did not have the benefit of history to show what would and would not have worked. Since we have the benefit of history since then, we can easily judge those designs for ourselves.

It's hard to image that in less than 70 years, mankind went from not being able to fly to landing on the moon. In the years since the moon landings, computers matured and became a viable technology. Aviation technology expanded very quickly for its first 50 years, but in the proceeding 60 years, it gave us huge jumbo jets and supersonic jets as well as helicopters capable of lifting heavy loads. In the last 60 years, computer technology was growing alongside it, again helping the aviation technology as well as every other technology it touched. This is an understanding that becomes the essence of this chapter as well as the book as a whole.

Clearly, the importance of understanding the history of the craft or study cannot be overstated. There is much to learn, not only from the direct history of the craft, but from the technologies that brought it into reality.

CALL TO ACTION:

When you embark on a new area of study or craft, seek out a system to use, study the history of the system as well as the systems that created it. Learn to understand how each of the various technologies evolved to create the new technology.

NOTES:

CHAPTER 13 - IT'S ALL ABOUT THE TRICKS/LEARNING TECHNIQUES

Learning to use finesse and techniques
will put us in the expert level on each task.

Our superpowers are unleashed with understanding. This book has focused on understanding from the way we learn, the systems we employ, and even the way the systems are constructed. I want to focus on why learning tips and tricks are important and how we gain experience. I want to discuss the importance of paying attention to the details. We want to avoid repeating bad habits and learn to identify those tips or tricks that are valuable to us and help gain techniques that only experience can give us. This is where you begin to really unleash your superpowers. For those who are facing a new career or job, gaining experience is the first challenge. Experience has value, but if you want to make your experience more valuable, you will learn to gather tips and tricks and learn new techniques. This is my favorite part of the process and the biggest challenge we face.

Experience comes from learning techniques

Tips and tricks gained by other mavens' experience are passed down, and some you will learn yourself as you continue to refine your craft or success system. Your long term success will depend on your ability to pick up on this simple but powerful trait. This will teach you how to get the expertise that takes others a lifetime to acquire. Many get caught up in doing the same thing over and over again without advancing. This means that bad habits are also repeated. Our plight is one of separation, separation of useful tips and tricks from bad habits, separation of experts from amateurs, separation of highly skilled from inexperienced, separation of understanding from misunderstanding, separation of successful from unsuccessful. Since failures are part of success, we must now learn how to leverage those failures in order the get to the success.

A chef friend of mine told me that he would rather get a new cook with little to no experience than one who has many years but a number of repeating bad habits. We have to remember that bad habits are what we seek to avoid. Learning new ways of doing things will aid us in our ability to mitigate repeating bad habits or inefficient skills. Learning to use finesse and techniques will put us in the expert level on each task.

My chef friend can walk you into the kitchen and without much thought give you tips like: use a given heat setting with a certain style pan, throw a little bit of basil in that sauce or do this to thicken or thin your sauce. For new cooks, not knowing how to do certain things becomes frustrating, but for the experienced chef like my friend, it is second nature. Let's say we are learning to become a chef. How we cut up an onion is important. Why? Because we are seeking the best practices, the tricks, the most efficient way of do things. How we cut up an onion may not seem important, but it all adds up. Learning about expert techniques is cumulative. If I can cut up an onion by changing a couple of cuts early, I can reduce the total number of times I have to bring my knife down. These add up. So the test is to use the least amount of time for the maximum consistency. Have you ever wondered why your favorite recipe comes out different each time? The answer is in the details. Cooking temperatures, measurements of ingredients, cooking times, even the order you put the ingredients together can affect the outcome of the dish. So in the interest of consistency and a quality product, you should pay as much attention to the details as you do to the larger items. This is where the evidence of the separation is obvious. The separation between the expert and the amateur, the one who can produce a good product and the one who can't, given the same recipe. If you watch cooking shows, you see that the bulk of the content they present is based on tips, tricks and techniques.

Experience is only as good as the techniques we acquire

Experience should never be measured in years or in any amount of time. Unfortunately, it happens to be the way our society measures it. I say unfortunately, because prison sentences are handed out in years and months, as well. Experience is only as good as how well one advances his or her craft and learns new techniques. In the large corporation where I worked, we had numerous employees in our IT department with various levels of expertise within the different areas of the business. One of the things I noticed is that just because someone has several years of experience in a certain discipline, that does not translate into proficiency. Also, even if someone has a certification, that does not mean he or she is equipped to handle the job like an experienced pro because training does not replace practical application. This is where the tips and tricks start to come in.

We had people in jobs that were a few years from retirement but had not advanced their craft in years. They were quick to point out how many years of experience they had as though it were something to behold. They might say they have 12 years' experience, when all they had was two years of advancing the craft and 10 years of repeating it. The reason this happens is not because they did not take classes or because they did not do the work, but rather that they did only what was necessary for that particular task and did not advance their craft or learn more proficient ways of doing their work. They were either apathetic or did not realize that their craft is a system which should continually be improved. It is a system of finding ways to do things better and of networking with others who are willing to share what they know. In our data center, we had people who wanted the technical documentation to be written in a recipe format. They wanted a step- by-step procedure. They followed these recipes each time they performed the task. If there was a problem, they would not know what to do and would have to call the next tier of support for help. They felt powerless to resolve the issue on their own. The way to combat this is through learning tips from other mavens.

Experience benefits from enhanced techniques

I have never encountered a craft that was at the end of its maturity cycle. All functions have room for improvement. Some processes within the craft have reached a level of maturity and efficiency, but there are still opportunities for improvement within the supporting processes. The refinement process came from my days as an automation developer. I understood that my job was not only to make the process more efficient, but also to create a process anyone could perform. By teaching computers the tricks and techniques, I was able to get it to complete the work for me. As a programmer, I learned that I could make changes to my code to create more efficient use of memory and machine cycles. There have been many instances when I was able to take a working program and tweak it or even rewrite areas of it to make it more efficient. The final product is a cleaner, less problem prone program.

Tips and tricks help us build techniques

The idea of using tips and tricks as means to get valuable experience seems like a simple and straight forward concept, yet there are those who excel at it and others who cannot seem to get started. If this chapter is going to be of value to you, I feel that it is important to share with you how I approach this. If I am engineer or even a Do-It-Yourself-er working on a solution that involves fabricating, the first thing to do is define the task or define what the outcome must look like. It may take several iterations to get it right, and I will talk about that in Chapter 15, but the first one is where I want to concentrate for now. Designing anything requires planning, and the design process is meant to flush out those things we need to work on. Part of the design process requires knowing what your capabilities are: this includes available materials, tools, skills, and facilities. After careful consideration and planning, you will realize there are several ways to accomplish the same goal. This is where the tips and tricks come into play. Some things are going to be straight forward and require little in the way of planning. However, you will eventually encounter an obstacle that may not be as clear cut.

The way we overcome those things is to consult other mavens personally, if available, or by reading articles or books, or watching YouTube videos. In all cases you are trying to find those helpful tidbits that will give you an edge when working on your project. You learn to discover techniques on your own. During this process, it is easy to establish some bad habits or practices that are less than optimal. This is a normal part of the process, unfortunately, so as a maven, we learn to identify when this begins to happen. It is easy to find the path of least resistance, and that is what we seek, but we also want to make sure the path is not encumbered with inefficiencies. The first time we do something we are just trying to make it work; the next time we see where we can improve. This is how tips and tricks are created. In support of the idea of transportable skills, we can consider that our learning finesse will increase our success, even on first time attempts at something. Over the years, I have gained a great deal of finesse, especially with mechanical skills. This finesse is what allows me to work on vehicles that I have never worked on before as a skilled mechanic. The techniques become transportable skills. The same technique used to work on one make will be the same for other makes of vehicles. Forming good habits as well as techniques will give you the confidence to take on projects you have never performed before. So, as a point of the tips and tricks is the ability to gain the finesse one must possess when doing things. This finesse is not limited to working on mechanical projects, either. I use a great deal of finesses when I write computer programs or when I am cooking. This finesse will give you a great deal of satisfaction.

I help a lot of people do a lot of things, but when I do, I do not just help them. I teach them. It is what mavens do. Not long ago I was helping a friend replace the brakes on his two mini-vans. Since the mini-vans were the same manufacturer and similar year models, the brakes on both vehicles were the same. The first rear wheel we completed took us almost 30 minutes. We had to deal with the e-brake and springs (drums). For each wheel we worked on, I studied the process and came up with a technique for improvement for the next wheel. By the time we dealt with the last wheel, we were able to do it in 7 minutes. Instead of simply repeating the mistakes and failures of the first attempt, I was able to take that improvement to the next wheel. We made a game of it, just to keep it interesting.

Tips and tricks are products of finding an efficient process

We have spent a lot of time talking about learning and how to gain the knowledge. We talked about being one who has tools and who can build tools, we talked about layers and systems and creating options. All of this culminates here. Not only will you know how to learn, but you will begin to teach yourself. This is the part of the process that can be the most rewarding. I suggest that each time you do a task, think about the task as though it were practice. As we hone the craft, we take each part of this as a learning experience. We seek a better way of doing it so that the next time we can complete the tasks not only quicker but better.

Eventually, we will begin to find the best approach to doing even the most menial task. This keeps our interest in it as well as making us more productive.

Another principle I want to discuss in the area of developing techniques is to do the task at least once. Since we know that failure is a part of success, we are going to find that the techniques that will stay with us are the ones we understand and successfully complete after our initial lack of success. In fact, if you have made several attempts with little or no success, a well timed tip will change everything for you. Any entrepreneur will tell you that success didn't happen the first time, or even the second. It is the perseverance and learning from your failures that pays off. Here is such a story: As a tool and die maker and ultimately a tool designer I saw all kinds of projects. The company I worked for hired some young engineers out of college to help in production. As a senior tool maker and CAD/CAM Programming Lead, I was responsible for making sure the tools were designed and built in a timely manner. One of these young engineers was given a project to design a production process for a new part that we were to produce. This included designing and building the tooling necessary. I had a great deal of respect for this young engineer, and I felt it helpful to pass along some helpful tricks from time to time. After looking at the part he was to produce, I realized that this type of part required some special knowledge of the way the tool had to be designed. I asked him if he knew how he was going to approach it. He gave me a brief description. I began to explain to him that he needed to pay special attention to certain features. He responded by telling me, "I want to see if I can figure this out on my own." I respected that he wanted to work it out using his own skills. I also knew that he would eventually get frustrated. I then told him, "When you get to the point where you need my help, let me know and I will be glad to tell you how that has to be done." He said, "Thanks. I will. Hopefully I won't have to." After he failed at several attempts, I realized he was headed in the wrong direction and would eventually be calling on me for help. The part was a seal that was made from a stock material that came in a roll. The part had to be completed at the installation because it went around another part. Since we had to deliver the part in its incomplete state to the customer, it was very important that the part fit as it should when it was to be installed. The engineer built a fixture that we used to test the design. He was having problems exactly in the area I knew he would. Later on, he finally relented and called me for help. After I explained why he was having the problem, I showed him how to overcome the problem. In this case, the instinct was to concentrate on the outside of the part, but it was the inside of the part that needed to be the focus. In any case, he followed my advice and the first attempt after that, he got it working perfectly, and the part fit, with the holes lining up and everything looking as it should. This engineer will remember this technique forever because he tried and failed several times prior to getting the answer he needed. I didn't just imagine the solution; I had to deal with it in the past with other tool makers, so I had the answer ready to go.

Tips and tricks are not always accepted by some

What I have learned from my interaction with people is that most are not as adaptable to this refinement concept as one might assume. Many people find it hard to change a system that has become so engrained to them. What appears to be a good technique to one person may not be evident to everyone. The challenge is to work through the various techniques and find the ones that actually work for you. Not all tips are useful just as not all techniques are worthwhile.

Not all processes can be changed due to restraints such as regulation and corporate rules, but, generally, small changes can be made. If you are a manager of people, seek out those who work toward refinement and do share their ideas with others. It is much better to build your teams around this concept than to build your team around someone who only looks good on paper.

Best practices are we seek

Now that I have driven you to this, it is time to put on the brakes a bit, too. While this approach to seeking the best techniques using tips and tricks is a great concept, be careful that it does not take over everything. Remember this is a process-- it is a method of gaining experience; it is not "the" experience. Keep in mind that not all ideas are good ones. This is why it is important to consult other mavens. This is also the reason you should think through the entire process, paying attention to the details. As you get more experienced with the transportable skills, you will start to identify those things that are worthwhile and those that are not. When working with a friend of mine, I get numerous suggestions on things we can do differently. Many of the ideas are ones I had already considered and was able to dismiss. Some, however, are good ones, and I will listen. When passing on tips and tricks, it is always best if you use a "Best Practice" approach.

In many of our team meetings in my previous position, I would have some lengthy and detailed debates with another maven on my team. This bothered some of our team members as they thought we were arguing and did not like each other. The truth is that we had a great deal of respect for one another. We really did value the opinions of the other. Our debating was really our way of filtering out each other's weak points to come up with the strongest process or best practice. If the process could stand up to each of our experienced objections, we knew that in the end, we had a workable process. We would often laugh about how people misunderstood our method.

Let's take a moment to review. Learning the tips and the tricks are how we hone our techniques. We are constantly seeking more efficient ways of honing the process, and that starts with some of the simplest processes. We do not want the constant enhancement process to be "the process." We are only attempting to refine the processes of our craft. We learn techniques from our less than successful attempts so we can pass them along for use in the future. We have to be ever vigilant, especially as managers, not to stifle this because we think we have all the answers. As managers, we owe it to our employers to make the process of refinement through improved techniques a part of our management style.

Within your local work group, opportunities to learn better techniques are all around you. Sometimes, we struggle with new members in the group who may not know about past issues and often they will want to re-fight old battles. There are battles you can fight, and there are battles you can win. As a process matures, these situations will come up more often. A challenge facing all mavens is the constant revisiting of old issues. As you become a mature maven, you will begin to recognize mature processes and borrow from them. Remember the chapters on transportability of skills? We want to transport the techniques from the mature process into new processes. You will start to understand the system and methods that got them there. You will find that your understanding of the layers will help you find the patterns that will allow you to borrow the techniques and use them in new ways to enhance your own processes. This is your new superpower!!! This is why I focused so much attention on this subject. Process improvement is the stated goals of every organization. A higher level manager once told a group of us, "If you don't like doing things the way we want, you may want to find another place to work." Do not be that person.

CALL TO ACTION:

Start to evaluate those things that you do on a daily basis, and learn to recognize some of the things you already do that can be considered a technique. Look at ways you can improve your technique. Look for opportunities to gain other techniques by applying some tips and tricks learned from others or the ones you develop personally.

CHAPTER 14 – CREATING A SUCCESS SYSTEM

A success system is built on strong
fundamentals and common traits.

We have covered some of the powers needed to unleash our superpowers, such as creating options, finding patterns, observing systems and fighting our biases. Now is when we start to unleash our superpowers. Being a maven is about making connections, and this chapter is about designing a success system by making connections to what we have learned and the process for creating new connections. When unleashing our power to succeed, we want to ensure that we are also working on ourselves. This discussion will be centered on a success system for a business or a brand, but remember a success system can be applied to all aspects of your life. This means the principles will also work for other success systems. As you learn to build and perfect your success system, you will be able to repeat this over and over again.

What is a success system?

A success system is a well designed system that will produce results leading to success. The reason you need a success system is because if you are not using one, one is being used on you. It is easy to understand why we need a good strategy in playing a game or in a military conflict. We want to recognize that success has to have a battle plan, as well. A success system is built on strong fundamentals and common traits. We can design our success system by finding models of existing success systems. A model that just provides for existence is not considered a success system unless your stated goal is simply to exist. A success system is not just about a sales pitch or a good product; it encompasses the entire enterprise or endeavor. In a success system, even the little things matter, so pay attention to the details. This is as true in the larger view as is it in the smaller view. History can be our best teacher of what a success system would look like, but past performance is no guarantee of future results.

Too many times we see businesses take the attitude of the "Field of Dreams." They convince themselves that "If you build it, they will come." Or, the adage: "Build a better mousetrap and the world will beat a path to your doorstep." History has proven that is a poor strategy for success. As you will see, it is important to have a good product; however, your success is not guaranteed by that. The road to success is littered with good ideas or good products that never found success. It may feel like it's better to be lucky than good, but relying on luck is a path to failure, as well. It really is better to have a success strategy.

System designs that work well can be reused, but a particular success system is not universal, nor does one size fit all. A success system gives you direction, vision, perspective and purpose. A solid success system is well constructed with properly formed layers or sub-systems. A success system must adjust to changing conditions. As a system analyst myself, I decided to explore what some of those traits are. In doing so, I created a blueprint for creating a success system or modifying an existing system.

A maven or strong leader at the nucleus

Whether we are talking about Thomas Edison, Steve Jobs, Sam Walton, John D. Rockefeller, Henry Ford or any of a host of others, each time we observe a success system, there was a single individual who created the nucleus of the system, driving the system. These mavens illustrate the need to perfect our systems and are the ones we try to emulate. So for that reason, our plight is to concentrate on ourselves as the implementer of the success system. As any entrepreneur will quickly attest, there is a lot of personal effort required to be successful.

The success system still requires a team effort, so the coach or maven must direct the success system. It is important to the success system to have qualified personnel that can carry out the system. The team may not need to understand the entire system. They do, however, need the skills to understand their subsystem and be capable of performing. It is easy to fall into the trap where family and friends are employed when they lack the skills necessary.

A clear definition of what success is

The very first thing we do in creating our success system is to define what a success is, recognize what success isn't. Setting goals is important to implementing a success system. Our success system requires a written statement that will serve as the foundational strategy for our system. We will call this a Success Statement. This statement will be the one consistent theme throughout.

We have seen "Mission Statements" used, but this will go beyond a mission statement. Some mission statements are well formed and can serve as a success statement. If your mission statement is not sufficient to meet this standard, then creating a fresh mission statement can serve both purposes. Businesses generally approach the goal setting portion of their business as a 'to-do' list, but this type of goal setting is not adequate in crafting a success statement.

A mission statement is normally published as part of your marketing campaigns. This is the impression you want your customers to get from you. However, a success statement may be one that you will want to keep private. This is totally up to you and your goals. An example of a mission statement may be "Satisfy our customers' needs by producing the best Product in the industry." This will work for customer relations, and you may, in fact, have that as a goal, but it really gives us little in the way of establishing a path to success. A success statement may be more clearly set as "Dominate the Widget Industry." Or, "Make the Widget Brand a household name." If you are a Mom and Pop shoe store in a world of Walmarts and other mega-retailers, you may want to set your success plans to something like, "Have 10 Mom and Pop brand shoe stores in the greater city limits." Success statements are not necessarily for public display. A lot of family success statements may look like "Get completely out of debt," "Put away enough for Junior's college." These are really part of a greater strategy of planning for a day when one can retire. It is never too soon or too late to establish a success statement.

As with patterns, the one with consistency is the fundamental pattern. Since this is a foundational goal, it will then be considered the first layer of our system. This is the layer all others are dependent upon. This definition of success should be like all goals: actionable, measurable and realistic. The statement of success should represent an outcome. Using a statement such as, "Make lots of money" is not a good statement of success since it is not clearly defined and can become illusive. The other problem with it is that making money is the life blood of any business, so it is an expected goal. While many corporations state that success is "To return value to the shareholder," that is not a sufficient enough goal since it is the same thing. I don't like any success statement that views success as anything slightly above existence. However, a statement such as," Build the Industry's Best widget, would be a better statement. It provides us a clear target and the by-product will achieve other non-stated goals. The goal must be measurable, so there must be a way to make sure you have achieved the goal. As you will soon see, a well-designed success system has many layers to it. It would be a good practice to create a statement of success for each layer in the system.

A good success system will meet or exceed its projected outcomes when applied properly. For that reason, a realistic target must be established. Success has many friends, while failure has few. Make your goals high enough to be meaningful but low enough that success can be celebrated. We don't want to create an unrealistic set of goals that will leave everyone frustrated.

A well designed success system with properly crafted layers

Start to describe your success system. This is the one area that may change over time. Remember, a success system must be flexible and adaptable over time. It must be all encompassing. The success system should include an endgame or an exit strategy. An example of that would include, taking your business public or selling the business. It may include passing the business to an heir or a trust. The exit strategy is an outcome of its own. You cannot see where you are going unless you have a target to reach. Remember, not all ideas are good ideas; sometimes the simplest and most elegant ideas are the best ones.

At this point, we have 3 primary layers to our system.

➢ The Foundational Objective -- Statement Of Success, how we define success

➢ Functional Layer – A large layer with several sub-layers within it. This is the working layer where we include product development, quality control, pricing, marketing and so on.

➢ Exit Strategy – The fruits of our success, expected final outcome.

A well designed success system will have several layers to it. There will be layers that are nested and those that cascade. From the chapter on layers, this is where this type of understanding is important. It is important in the design to ensure that the system is well thought out. Spend some time on this phase; you will start to see that planning at this early stage will benefit you through the entire process. This allows the system scale as needed. This also gives us priority to those layers upon which the others are dependent.

Each layer should have its own statement of process; likewise, so should each sub-layer. The statement or process will describe the layer's role, expected outcomes, responsibilities and interfaces. This will force you as the designer to make sure you have not duplicated processes. This will force you to keep your perspective. It will also allow you the opportunity to create growth areas for scaling your business. Your success system must include a plan for growth, when to grow and how to grow. Later, I will cover finding dynamic vs. static limitations, so your growth plans should also include a statement of process.

With each sub-layer there may also be sub-layers. How we define success will depend upon the measurable(s) or metrics. If we are looking at a product, how are we to determine if it is successful? Is it by the number produced? How good it is? Is it by the customer satisfaction with it? Is it based upon how many people know about it? You see, there are numerous ways to define success.

Someone looking at a sound mixing console notices all the knobs and wonders why there are so many knobs. Some of the controls are slide controls, and others twist. There are a number of display meters. Some look the same as the rest. At first glance, it may seem that the mixer is just a bunch of redundant knobs and gauges. If we start to understand what each one of them does, we soon see that this is a layered system with sub-layers. The relationship between the layers is one-to-many. Each one of the channels has its own control while there are controls for overall output. This type of control gives the technician flexibility to control the total output and each channel as necessary. A well designed success system will have the same features.

No single layer can be a point of failure. As you begin to implement your success system, be sure to pay attention to all the layers. An inefficient layer will prevent overall success. It doesn't matter how good a product is--if the marketing layer fails to perform, the rest of your success system fails along with it. For that matter, the system must work from beginning to end, the entirety of the flow of business. This all adds up to making sure your success system design is a global view. It is too easy to concentrate on those things we like doing or are comfortable with. A success system is all encompassing.

Keeping integrity in the system

You need a method for maintaining integrity. There is no success system that can prosper in the face of poor integrity. This section deals with making sure there is a code of ethics that is understood and maintained. If your success system relies on deceiving others, your system is a despotic system and deserves to fail. A clear establishment of conduct has to be created and then understood by all who are part of your system. If you believe that those whom you choose to be part of your system already know what the code of ethics is, you are making a huge mistake.

Outlining and documenting your code of ethics are an important part of creating your success system. Making sure all those involved understand these rules is equally important. There will always be those who will try to test these rules, so part of the establishment of these rules of conduct is what the consequences will be when they are violated. Also, the simple appearance of an ethical breach can be just as damaging to your system. Even if there is not a specific rule, it needs to be understood that an appearance of unethical behavior cannot be tolerated. Conflicts of interest are hard to define but are easily understood. Well-meaning gifts, for example, can be mistaken as "pay for play" activities. Having these rules will help prevent such things as pillaging of products both physical and service-based. Intellectual property must also be protected with this type of code. You outline what is acceptable for public knowledge and what is not. You create an environment in which those involved understand the need to protect information. That includes client information, both private and company related. You also make sure it is understood who owns the intellectual property.

If you have dress codes or other standards you are trying to uphold, this is the place to establish this. This step also enforces a compliance with any regulatory commission or agency. It also serves to protect your system. By applying some due diligence, this also provides you a means to document or how it shall be documented in the case of any legal actions.

You do not want to spend all the resources you have to build a system that someone either unknowingly or knowingly destroys. While this step can be easily overlooked, it carries a great importance that cannot be overstated. These steps will protect your system as well as aid in conflict resolution.

Success systems are dynamic; they can change over time and by region.

One of the key features of a well designed success system is that it can change as outside forces change. A success system that worked well in the 1970's may not work in the 2010's. Technologies, buying methods and quality of products have changed. Furthermore, as success systems are adopted by more of the marketplace, they lose effectiveness and uniqueness and. Thus, need refreshing. We have learned a lot about consumers over the years. With each passing generation, a new set of success models has to be created. Some of the basic building blocks will never change those that appeal to our human nature. Attitudes change and that results in different buying habits.

In the discussion about layers, I talked about the importance of flexible layers. Not all layers may require changing. This furthers the point about the need to monitor results. For that reason, even if we are using a dated success system, some simple tweaks may be all that is necessary to fix the overall system. It may be that the fundamentals of your success system are still relevant and strong, but a tweak in the marketing layer could be adjusted. Timing is important, as demonstrated when Steve Jobs had to wait to bring out the iPad until after the iPhone was established. The market's attitude toward the device had changed, so had the technology. His success system planned for this, but what often happens is that we get blindsided by such changes.

Learn the importance of tools.

One of the things that differentiate humans from other animals is our ability to create and use tools. In the chapter on options, we discussed why tools are important. A success system requires tools. We talked about the benefit of having general purpose tools; here we want to focus on why specific tools are important, as well. Throughout history, mankind has never reached a point where technology has stopped. There have been slow-downs, but the trends were always toward more sophisticated tools. We have to be mindful of this trend in our success system design. If we are not using adequate tools, then someone else certainly will. Tools come in all forms; this includes hand tools, power tools, software tools, online tools, vehicles, and so on. We need to take a complete inventory of our tools so as to see how to best utilize them. Efficiency is at the heart of why we own and use tools. Be sure you keep that perspective.

We need to find the value in those things we use or need to purchase. A success system leverages all the tools it has to their fullest potential. While the concept of first mover's advantage has its place in the area of tools, we don't want to find ourselves on the "bleeding edge" either. When we evaluate our tools, we want to make certain that the costs of the tools are justified. Here is an application of that point. In today's world, businesses are compelled to have a web presence. A website for many businesses is nothing more than an electronic brochure. This is an application of a likely underutilized tool. Today's customer expects more from websites than just a simple page of information. The web-page is quickly becoming the initial contact point for customers; it needs to capture as well as provide information. As with any tools you have, fully utilizing its capabilities will help build a solid success system.

I have witnessed systems where the philosophy was to buy as many tools as could be financed. While this philosophy understands the value of having tools, it loses the value of the tools by overpaying for them or not having the options of finding the best value in them. Being tool poor is not a design for an effective success system. Contrast that with an opposing philosophy where there is reluctance to purchase more sophisticated tools. This philosophy fails to see the trade-off that comes with not having sufficient tools. You can pay for tools many times their costs by trading time or labor to do the same job as the proper tools could do for you.

Automation has proved its value many times over when properly applied. In the discussion of automation, it is important to bring up this point. The promise of automation is not to remove people from the process, but to level the playing field so that unskilled workers can be as efficient as the skilled workers and with greater consistency. This is not just a principle in computer automation but in all processes. We develop tools around the techniques that are learned from experience.

The information system includes all the information

When most small businesses think about their information systems, they naturally focus on their computer systems. Since the 1960's, we have been conditioned to understand that data processing means computer systems. While our computer systems are central to our information system, we must not forget that our information system includes the entirety of our business's information. When you analyze a success system, it is easy to overlook this point. In fact, we become so focused on our computer-based information system that we fail to recognize the information that lives outside the computer systems.

Your paper files are part of your information system. Your forms, letters, emails, receipts, phone bills, business cards, contact information, hand written notes, quotes, warranties, service manuals, and so on, are all part of your business information system. Computers automate the gathering and retrieval of information. The most effective systems are the ones that dovetail together. What this means is that when you introduce an automated software solution into your business, you should not fail to adjust your non-digital system to leverage the automation.

Here is a situation the may exist: Your business purchases a new G/L accounting system, and within the system there is an inventory, accounts receivable, and accounts payable. Your business still maintains a large body of paper files that includes sales orders, notes and so on. There is another group of files that contain part information such as detailed part information. The part information is sorted based on a part number, while the sales order information is by date. The computer can give us the information in any number of ways. The best filing system will be one where the related information is co-located. This means when you go to the drawer, all the information can be gathered at one time. Some filing systems require you to move from different cabinets to get all the information. The files can now be given a file number that the computer can easily dispense with so that if you need to file the some papers, a simple query from the computer will send you to the exact location where most, if not all, the information can be gathered.

In today's business world it's easy to think that just because you have a computer, you have automated the information. Nothing can be farther from the truth. We see so many of our documents going paperless that the assumption is that we have an efficient means of managing the information. It is easy to get lost in the endless emails and shared documents that can exist on our networks. If the files on our computer networks are not well organized and maintained, our system is no better than a paper system. Large folders full of various files can be as cumbersome as piles of paper on our desk. Part of your information system includes the files on your computer and network. These files deserve to be managed in an organized fashion. In other words, stop putting all your files on your computer's desktop. That defeats the purpose of having a computer in the first place.

Technology has given us all a huge gift. Businesses are some of the largest benefactors to it. Our plight is to recognize all of what it offers and take as much advantage as possible. Learn the relationships that exist between and within your data. A well designed database is considered to be normalized. All your system's data should be normalized, if not in a database, at least in the form following the rules of normalization.

Learn to understand those things that are static and those that are dynamic.

In everything we encounter in life, there are those things over which we have control and those over which we don't. We can categorize these things into 2 groups: Dynamic and Static, which are the easiest ways to evaluate things. A good success system takes into account these things in an effort to avoid certain situations and to try to concentrate on those things we can benefit from the most. Examples of static things come in the form of rules or regulations, due dates, environmental issues, resources, hours in a day, location of your business, and the list goes on from there.

If your business is a restaurant, for example, you are limited by supply of certain food products, number of tables for seating, your kitchen's ability to cook food, and business hours. You will want your success system to take advantage of the things you can control to get the best yield from those things that limit you. This concept is true in all success systems. For the restaurant business, takeout orders represent a dynamic component which can fully utilize the kitchen's ability to produce. A finite amount of tables for seating or capacity limitations and a narrow serving window of time can max out your potential for success rather quickly. In the food service business, the most successful systems are the ones that service take out or drive through business. This model allows for full advantage over a service business that only caters to direct seating.

We want to look at those things that are dynamic or infinite. A baseball team has a limit of 3 outs per inning and 9 innings per game. The team can produce an infinite number of runs within those constraints. If you build your strategy around trading 1 run per out, you are creating a limitation on your team. The constraints limit your production if you do not develop a system that takes full advantage of the dynamic components within your system. If you are a business that has a service product, you will be constrained by hours within a day, so you must find a way to offer products with an unlimited sales option.

Constraints can change over time. Technology removes constraints, laws change, what was once a constraint may not be as big a constraint. Constraints can kill your success system, especially if you cannot adjust to the changes. All systems will have constraints, so knowing what they are and planning for changes will give you the best leverage.

The valuation of a good product

At the center of every business is a product. This product can be an item or service. For this discussion, a product includes anything you sell. Having a good product is always a requirement for a business success system. In order to get the most value from the product you are selling, you need to make sure the product has value. The way this is accomplished is by returning value to the customer. Having a good quality product is a great place to start. Having a quality product saves you on returns and wasteful defects. Quality control has to be incorporated in such a way as to protect you and your customer from annoying problems. It will also create customer loyalty, satisfaction and overall good will. Your customer's satisfaction with your product will make your brand or break it. Since we are concentrating on creating a success system, it is imperative that the customer get value from the product for the selling price.

I must be understood that you are ultimately responsible for the price of the product you are selling. While factors such as supply and demand will affect the price of any product, your role is to insure that value is always achieved. If you have properly managed the static and dynamic components in your product, your success system has to include a method for gaining value. However, value is always perceived, and that perception of value gives you the most leverage. This is the reason why 2 similar quality and available products can have differing price points. The customer's perception of value will allow you to get more for your products. As in the restaurant example above, convenience or atmosphere can affect this perception. Therefore, establishing a price that is targeted to the correct demographic will allow you to get the optimum price for your product. Keep this thought in mind; a higher priced item will attract a more affluent demographic. If you price your product too cheaply, the perception that it is an inferior product could result.

If you are developing a product, here are some points you should consider. You are ultimately building a brand. The perception of the brand will drive your level of success. Customer loyalty is really the goal of any success system. For that reason, I suggest that you create a platform, not just a product. This may be difficult to understand, so think of it like this: Apple has created what many consider to be an eco-system. This means that all their products dovetail easily with each other. An Apple customer will find it easier to stay with the Apple brand rather than mix and mingle the products. This approach should be driven by quality control rather than simply locking in a customer. If you use the platform to simply force customers to stay with your product, you could experience a backlash, so your platform must accommodate competitive products, as well. Your platform will have a set of intangibles; these are the things that make your product unique so as to create a value no one else can provide. Here are some examples of some successful platforms:

- Facebook – Social Website

- eBay – Online Auction Site

- Windows – Microsoft Operating System (Personal Computers)

- Wal-Mart – Superstores and neighborhood markets

- Google – Search engine and online services

- Amazon – Book seller and online market place

- Netflix – Video content delivery

In each of these platforms, the product is provided by someone else. The platform is established by giving the consumer access to products. Sure, these platforms may provide some of their own branded products, but that is not the focus of the platform. Microsoft Windows is literally a software platform that allows various software applications to run on it. Even Microsoft Office provides a suite of tools that give the users the ability to build on it. Keeping this in mind, another characteristic of a platform is that it becomes a building block and a way for forward growth.

As a platform vs. just a product, you will create a draw for your customers. Your customers will begin to seek you out as their place to find what they are looking for. To further define what a platform is, consider that you have a suite of products that have a tie together in such a way that the products within the suite support the other products. The suite or platform may not include a total solution, but it will give the customer the means to build to a total solution. Your goal for the platform is to provide enough of the solution that the customer wants to stay within the means of the platform. Even if your products are not all inclusive in the platform, having the means to include third party products will create the customer loyalty and satisfaction that will provide long-term success. The most important goal of any platform is to solve a problem for the customer. The more seamless you can make the products work together within the platform, the more loyal your customer.

Your platform should have both entry level and high end products. You want to attract the value buyers because you will turn them into loyal customers. The lower end product will add value to the higher end products, as well. The consumer market is the lower end market for a lot of companies' products. There are professional quality products that are designed for the professional for a higher price. When you build a product, you will keep in mind that a lower end product will serve as a means to pay for overhead and production; the higher end product will pay for development costs. Having a range of products from lower to higher will allow you to move products from the higher end to the lower end as the product matures. This will also provide you with the valuable economy of scale. The lower end product will provide volume where the higher end will create cash flow for the development of the next generation of the product. There are some consumers who will buy the more expensive product based on the perception that it is much better than the lower priced product.

As your success system's maven, you have to be the futurist, the one who sees past today and looks toward the promise of tomorrow. As we look back through history and begin to analyze those who got it right and those who missed the mark, we can find a trend that we all need to strive for. The trend is of course, "understanding." The futurist who had the best or clearest understanding of the technology knew what the technologies would bring. It is easy to get caught up in the Hollywood version of the future or, as in the 1990's dot-com era, we tend to not consider the technology as much as the fantasy of the technology. In order to find the future of any technology, it is very well to look at the history and the core problem it was designed to solve. Today, with the proliferation of computers in our lives, we have lost many of the core understandings of what the computer was designed to do. Stay focused on those things that are real about the technology. Study the problems it solved historically, but don't buy into the hype. Understand those things that have caused it to evolve in an effort to realize where the next evolutionary trend will be.

Learn to ask questions

We have all answered market surveys generally designed to find out specific information about demographics, advertisements, and product satisfaction. When I suggest that you learn to ask questions, you should consider surveys. However, when you are developing a product or trying to solve a problem, it is much better to know what the actual problem is you are trying to solve. In cases where clients come to you and tells you what they want, they are telling you what they perceive the solution to be. The reality is, they are asking you to solve their problem. In this case, it is vitally important to understand the nature of the problem they want solved. This may require asking more questions. The most important thing you must do is to listen. What happens next is the problem will be best stated outside of a Q/A session.

A conversation about what keeps the customer up at night or what are his or her biggest concerns will tell you more about the problem, if you know how to listen. Your clients will sometimes imagine a solution that they have conceived based on their own perception of limitations. I cannot tell you how many times I have been told that something could not be done when I know from experience that it can be done. It is human nature to see solutions through our own understanding. It is incumbent on mavens to understand not only the solution, but understand the problems your client is facing. The most elegant of solutions are the simplest ones, but the best solutions solve the problem now and for the foreseeable future. Solving problems is at the heart of what gives mavens their strength.

In the late 1950's, data processing systems were coming on the scene. These systems were big, slow and expensive. Only larger companies and governments could afford them. In 1959, IBM introduced the 1401, which was priced low enough for medium to large businesses. This was the first transistor-based computer and would allow programs to be stored in memory vs. hard-wired panels. It was faster and smaller than the earlier models. This computer was a huge success. For businesses, buying or leasing the computer was only the beginning. Programs had to be custom written. Businesses investing in technology found this system a good place to start. This was the model-T of business computers, however...

Computer companies were more focused on building faster and better computer processors, so they lost sight of what businesses needed. There was the perception that if you built a faster computer and sold it cheaper, then you would capture the market. This was true to a large extent; however, businesses had bigger problems. At the time, business needs outpaced the resources of these data processing systems. Upgrading was a constant concern. Computer manufacturers were making great strides; unfortunately, a machine was often obsolete before it was in full production.

The business customers found themselves with a problem - each new system required new software, and compatibility was a huge issue. A few IBM managers listened to, and understood the problems facing their customers and decided to solve their problem. IBM had to stop and re-evaluate some of its priorities with respect to new systems. It decided that it would create a common instruction set along with common peripheral interfaces. The IBM 360 was introduced in 1964. This new computer system was a huge advancement in data processing. It would allow customers to leverage their earlier investments of hardware and software like none before it. This is a situation where the customers did not know what the answer was; they would have believed they were constrained by things they did not understand. Some forward thinking managers at IBM solved the problem at a great deal of expense, but it was worth it. This single action changed the face of data processing and created what we now call the software industry. For the first time, customers' investments in software could be carried forward. This allowed upgrades to become as simple as unplugging old equipment and replacing it with new equipment. It was a huge success for IBM, making it the leader in that industry. Needless to say, asking questions and listening to your customer is vital to any success system.

Marketing your product or service

Your success system must include a marketing plan. When you develop a marketing plan, you have to consider your target demographic. While this seems like common sense, it has to be mentioned. More important than simply using an advertising media to target your demographic, you must turn your advertisement into a message your customers will want to see. Nothing will cause your customers to lose interest faster than forcing them to consume messages they are not interested in.

When it comes to marketing your product, you have to stand out from the crowd. You have to get the customer's attention. One of the easiest ways to gain a customer's loyalty is to make his or her job easier. If you are forcing your customer to do all the research as to why buying your product is a good decision, you will lose that customer to someone who does the work for them. This does not mean that you overload your customer with information, quite to the contrary. If you are selling to CEOs, for example, their needs are specific. Everyone needs reassurances that they are making the right buying decisions. A CEO will need to see a "Return on Investment (ROI)". A CEO is an investor, and to be a disciplined investor, you will supply him or her with the information that allows for making prudent investment decisions. Contrast that with an engineer who is solving a very different problem. An engineer will need technical specifications, not just hype. If you are targeting a young demographic, you will want your advertisement to be current to the times. If you are selling to an older demographic, you will not use words that they may not understand. It is important to understand what your customer's needs are and how best to communicate your solution will serve them.

In today's world, a business website is a must. The website should be easily navigable, including closing the sale, providing promotional materials, capturing contact information, and giving access to information that your customer needs. In other words, it should be much more than just a fancy brochure. You website should look professional; after all, it will become the face of your business. Even if you have a brick and mortar business, the online presence is more than just an extension. It is the main communication vehicle for your business. The website should be compatible with mobile computing devices. You will want to consult someone who specializes in best practices for websites. Building your own website will save you money, but if you are unable to convert visitors into sales, it will cost you money, especially if you are paying for advertising for your website. Your conversion rate is the easiest place to get the best value for your advertising dollars. If you don't see the value in what a website can provide your business, you're not working within a success system.

Your advertising should tell your story. You want your customer to know why you are the expert. The more your customers feel that you are qualified to provide the product, the more willing they will be to allow you to. Your story can include the history of your business or your own personal background. You should give examples of how you solved other customers' problems. The way you present your products will come down to the simple principle: It's a good decision to buy your product. You will want to tell your customers that. Give them permission to buy your product.

You should be where your customer is, or expects to find you. Location is as important to some businesses as the product is. A fast food restaurant will need to be easily accessible and clustered with other fast food restaurants. A car dealer will do best when located near a high traffic area. A tractor dealer will need to be in a rural community. Location is extremely important; it can make or break a business, so you will want to make this a priority.

Details are important. Even the little things matter.

Even the little things matter. That includes how you represent yourself in your advertisements as well as how you treat your customers. Don't forget to pay attention to the details in every aspect of your success system. Remember this important point - a success system is all inclusive.

Businesses survive on revenue. It all adds up. If you overspend on expenses, you have to make that up in revenue. As a business, everything you spend money on has to be treated as an investment. Things like tax planning and travel expenses have to be viewed the same way. Make sure not to spend a $1.00 to save $0.75. That is an easy trap to fall into. Likewise, spending a $1.00 to make $1.15 may not be the best use of resources. Resources are what make a business work. Remember that there are static expenses and dynamic expenses. Be certain to leverage everything to its best yield. To be sure, time is the most valuable resource. Make certain that you are not trading hours for dollars since hours are static and dollars are dynamic.

Companies can put too much value in things of little value. An example would be when you spend $100.00 a month to store product that is only worth a couple of thousand. How many months of storage will it take to pay for that product again and again? This is the philosophy that gave us "JIT" or "Just In Time" inventory systems. In the interest of paying attention to the details, avoid becoming so bogged down in the details that it becomes counterproductive.

Where systems fail to be success systems

We have discussed what we need to design a success system. Now, let's shift gears and talk about those things that will prevent us from having a success system. Optimization is the key to a good performing success system. This includes everything from the employees to the products to the price at which we sell them.

1.   Don't pay more for the product than you sell it for. This sounds simple, but it is not. The cost of goods sold should include all the costs; that is, production, sales, inventory, and taxes are all components that make up the cost of goods sold. If you are selling products for less than they cost, you should raise your prices, lower your cost or end that part of the business.

2.   Don't allow systems within your business to masks other problems. This is another one of those traps. Each subsystem within your success system should be evaluated to insure that it is not covering up problems that need to be addressed. The inventory example is a good one. Companies will keep too much inventory, thinking it gives them an advantage, when it really hides the fact that they don't do a good job of planning or managing their resources.

3.   Make sure you sell what you produce or buy. I can buy automotive products from Wal-Mart, but only those things that move in a timely manner. I am not able to buy products specific to my classic car from Wal-Mart because the market is too small for the volume they target. If you have a business that is specific to a type of

market, you will need to understand your market very well. Have alternate sources, allowing you to leverage, acquiring only the products that you will be able to sell.

4. Staying with an old and outdated success system will eventually cost more than it produces. Technology has changed the face of business as well as our personal lives; learn to leverage technology anywhere you can. Remember, if you don't, your competition will. An example would be buying a large inventory of printed materials such as manuals, sales brochures, and training materials. In today's world, print on demand services will keep your costs down and allow you more flexibility. There is something to be said for a proven system, but as with all things, they, too, have a shelf life. Don't be the last business using an out-dated success system.

Success Systems are not an accident.

Keep in mind when you develop your success system that it takes thought and planning. Success systems don't just happen. On rare occasions, some products reach a level of success due to the market demand and a lack of competing product. Those products are short lived and rare. Understand that the only way to insure a level of success is through a diligent, well planned and constructed, efficient, dynamic success system.

CALL TO ACTION:

Design a success system of your own. Start with a statement of success. Practicing this trait will help you even on small projects.

---

12 Key points for your success system:

1. A success system should be well planned with a definition of success.

2. All parts of the system should have a plan, don't leave things to chance.

3. Create a platform, a product suite designed to work together to solve a problem

4. Product suite should include a professional version and a consumer line

5. Your success system should be flexible, ready and able to adjust to changing markets

6. Know your customers, know what they struggle with, know how to reach them.

7. Your success system must be committed to integrity

8. Focus on the right tools for the efficiency that they offer

9. Your information system include all information and should be handled accordingly

10. Identify those things that are static and those things that are dynamic

11. Your products value to the customer is your responsibility.

12. Your marketing needs to explain why your product has value to the customer.

CHAPTER 15 - IMPLEMENTATION OF GOALS

As new capabilities are created, several
dependencies may be resolved.

When I talked about designing your success system, I talked a lot about setting goals and of having a good plan. If you have been paying attention, we are establishing a system. Developing a product or completing goals follows a system, as well. This chapter discusses what steps one must go through to take a concept or a project to a finished product. You can also apply this to solving problems or accomplishing your goals. The relationship between goals and projects is this: a project is that task that has to be performed or product that has to be produced, and the goal is the point at which one can acknowledge success has been achieved.

Goal setting establishes the scope

There are numerous books on setting goals and setting them up so that they are attainable, actionable, realistic, and measurable. There are white papers, articles, books, seminars and such, teaching you how to set goals. They focus on helping you in the crafting of the goals so that you will be successful. However, in this chapter, I will teach you the system, the process or the formula used to accomplish the goals. It's one thing to document the goals, it is quite another to accomplish the goal. The value in setting goals, whether it is a project or task, is to manage the scope.

This formula works whether we are talking about a project, a goal, or even a small task. The process is similar in each. To distinguish the difference between a project, goal or task has to do with reach or scope. A project has a larger scope than a goal, and a goal has a larger scope than a task. Tasks build the goals; the goals build the project.

Describing the outcomes

We start with the broadest category, the project. In our documenting of the project, we use broad terms to describe it. Now, the important thing to remember here is that we are talking about outcomes. This is different than simply giving the project a name. This is where we describe what the project is designed to accomplish. This includes a definition of what the project is. For example, I have a project to automate a process. We have to define when the process begins and when the process ends. What constitutes the process? What do we mean by "automate?" There are various levels of automation, from slightly automated to highly automated. What benefit are we expecting? The documentation process of the project gives us the scope of the project. It will help us with determining the costs and benefits of the project. It will also allow us to keep the scope under control. Scope creep is where the project begins to go in new directions from the original intent. I will address this more, later in this chapter.

Establish the workflows

Once the project is documented, we establish a work-flow. This is when we start establishing a set of goals within the project. In order to get a proper work-flow we must plan the way the project is to be implemented. At this stage, we will want to begin to list those processes that we know we need to accomplish. Next, we want to create a list of dependencies. A dependency is anything process-wise, material-wise, facility-wise, tool-wise or personnel-wise that can prevent the goal from being reached. This part of the project planning and goal setting is called "resolving the dependencies." This is as important as any other step because it will influence the priorities. Keep in mind we are looking for everything to flow as the project develops. Priorities are there to keep us on task. We need to establish a list of those things that we can do. This is the opposite of the dependency; this is where we understand our capabilities. Capabilities are not limited to a process; they also include tools, facilities, materials and other sources. This is where your maven superpowers are starting to pay off.

Resolving dependencies with capabilities

In the area of resolving dependencies, we want to consider that things change, materials change, our tool inventory changes, our skills change, and technology changes. In fact, the only constant in life is change. Therefore, we are always vigilant to look at those things that were once thought to be a dependency that may no longer be. Our capabilities will change as we reduce the amount of dependencies. In the chapter on success systems, I mentioned finding those things that are static and dynamic. Dependencies are part of that discussion, as well. We have dependencies that are tied to static situations, so the dynamic situations can influence both the capabilities and dependencies.

To further clarify a dependency, we will want to look at

some examples. If I am building a cabinet, the dependencies that I may have would be the following: design requirements, materials and tool availability, facility for assembly, installation restrictions, finishes required, miscellaneous hardware and transportation. In each of the above dependencies, some may be easy to overcome while others may not be. It is the dependencies that are hardest to overcome that must be focused on as a priority. Since each of the dependencies can jeopardize the entire project, it is incumbent upon us to have a plan or a process to overcome them. If, in the process of discovering and identifying the dependencies, we determine that the design has to change, then we will want to identify that early. For example, if at the installation site for the cabinet, it requires that the finished pieces must fit through a door opening, we will want to design the cabinet in such a manner as to provide for onsite assembly where the pieces fit through the door opening.

We will begin to see the previously unforeseen dependencies at this point. The goal of this process is have forethought enough to at least understand what is required. We also want to minimize the unforeseen dependencies as a working process in the pursuit of completing our tasks, leading to the success of the project. This process may require several iterations or back and forth attempts until a solution has been reached. As we resolve a dependency, we may encounter new ones that were previously unforeseen. Likewise, as new capabilities are created, several dependencies may be resolved. Therefore, it is important to look at capabilities based on the number of dependencies they will resolve. Capabilities expand as we resolve the dependencies. We must identify our capabilities based on application. Application of capabilities will determine our success.

Application drives the platform

This principle is central to our discussion. Application drives the platform. What do I mean by "platform?" Just as we discussed in the Success System chapter, a platform is what the solution will be based upon. So, it makes no sense to decide on a platform without fully understanding the application. I wouldn't ask a cabinet shop to build a car. It may not even be well suited to build a house, but if I want a piece of custom furniture, the cabinet shop would be able to accommodate that type of project. As simple as this seems in theory, we must have a good understanding of the application as a dependency for deciding on a platform. If you haven't figured out by this time I talk quite a bit about systems and those things that build the system that could easily be said for the use of platforms. I want to get you, as the reader and as a person who wants to become a maven, to start learning to identify how powerful the understanding of these constructs can be.

Watch for scope creep

As we examine our project, we have to pay attention to the scope. We discussed earlier that scope creep is a real possibility. This means that the process of resolving dependencies has become such a focus that it begins to take over the entire process. We want to ensure that the outcomes we documented in the early stages are being met. If we find that scope creep is beginning to take root, we must then stop and look at the platform we are using. This means that the application was too much for the platform. This entire discussion may seem to be a bit esoteric. Just remember this is all very general and that each situation will be different, but the essence is still the same. Understanding the fundamentals will help you when you take on a complex project. Understanding how to break down this process will give you the courage to take on these projects. Then, you will have unleashed your maven "superpowers."

Producing a product

Let's start with this idea that we are going to produce a product. This product may be your own idea, or it could be one that you are being paid to develop. In either case, we use the same approach. Let's consider that we are developing a product for the consumer market, generally understood to be the market with a mass appeal. The market is based on end users who are using their own personal funds to purchase, so the product has to be affordable and a good value.

With very few exceptions, most consumer products are the result of a maturing technology that we developed in the professional market place first. Video cameras were once the exclusive territory of news media and TV production studios. Today, we can make videos from our Smart Phones. You may have heard the saying that "Racing improves the breed." This refers to auto racing and how it has benefited the average driver. There is example after example of how professional technologies make their way down to the consumer market. Imagine what our lives would be like had the personal computer not been available to the consumer market. The lesson here is that we can take lessons from professional technologies as a transportable knowledge and apply it in the consumer market for our product development.

We can now establish a goal of performance and price for our product. Why start there? If we cannot make the product at an affordable price, then we are, by definition, not making it available to the consumer market. If, however, we can deliver on both performance and price, we have created value to the consumer, and that is what drives the market. In the search for price and performance, the type of materials used will play a huge role. In fact, the process of producing, the tooling and the machinery are all directly affected by the materials we use.

Next, you need to consider the number of units to be produced. If the product is highly specialized for the high-end consumer market, then you will only produce a small number; however, if the product will be in every household or automobile or computer system, you will need to plan for a larger production number. Design will be affected by the numbers to be produced because the tooling and process will be affected by it.

Let's look at our goals. We have established a lofty goal of creating a consumer product. We have intermediate goals of deciding on materials, manufacturing processes and tooling, but we have the issue of price and performance.

The best course of action for someone faced with this is to do some research. Find out all you can about the professional product you are emulating. Many times, plastics will work very well where some metals are used by the pros. Consumers don't give the heavy use a professional would, so a cheaper material will work many times to get the price in range.

If your consumer product does not have a professional counterpart, consider that most consumers will find that product to be gimmicky or unproven. Consider making a professional counterpart yourself for a higher price that can fund your development and the consumer will take it seriously. For most consumers, knowing that a professional product is available will make them trust the product category even more. Most large manufacturers such as Matsushita, GE, GM and Ford will produce higher level products to support the less expensive ones. This is also part of creating a platform for your products.

After you have accomplished the intermediate goals of price and performance, then materials and process, you now want to concentrate on building your first prototype. Remember, this unit should not be considered production; this is a learning exercise only.

Proof of concept and prototype stages

As we progress to our lofty goals, we are facing numerous intermediate goals, with the dependencies having a higher priority. We are going to build using a total of 5 prototype stages. These are not production pieces; therefore, they are independent goals. The later prototypes are dependent on the earlier ones. This means that you do not start building prototype stage five without having completed prototype stages one through four. Why the independence from one to the next? You will be saving yourself a lot of lost time and material if you do not produce products that will be obsolete before they are finished.

➢ The first prototype stage is a proof of concept

version. In fact, until you have a working prototype, you cannot count this stage as anything but the first one. This one's goal is to make it work while performance will come later. We must have a starting point.

➤ The second prototype stage is a refinement version. After you have used the first prototypes and looked at them and your processes, you will begin to see areas where you can improve, so the second stage proves the refinement.

➤ In the third prototype stage, you will know what you are going to keep and what you are going to work on. You can now begin to develop tools such as fixtures or bending dies or simple hand tools. This is also the point at which you can validate the performance. Enhancements at this level may take several cycles to complete. This is the test mule stage. Here is where we proof of concept our ideas and we get a clear vision of what the final product will look and perform like.

➤ In the fourth prototype stage, your tools and processes are maturing and any changes to design and materials are getting further refined. The fourth stage prototypes should closely resemble the production product and the production processes.

➤ The fifth prototype stage is a proof of process; it should be completed as a test of the entire process. The fifth prototype stage would be your first production stage. The first prototypes will most certainly look nothing like the fifth stage prototypes, but the fifth stage will give us what our true cost structure will look like.

If you have noticed, each generation or prototype stage is only connected by the knowledge, process and tools to the previous. This forces the growth and maturity of the product. As you can see, maturing the process is an important part of product development. If you stick with a formula such as this, you will turn out good products that the consumer values. You can use this same process when you are tasked with creating a new product, but the next generation will also follow the previous pattern. The next generation product should be treated as a new product.

As we approach each goal, we have smaller goals created from solving problems. This layering approach will drive your project and goals to completion because it naturally creates a project work flow. It gives us a path or an understanding of what has to happen next. A maven becomes accustomed to approaching problems in a programmatic way to ensure success.

CALL TO ACTION:

With each project you start, no matter how small, take the approach that you will prioritize your processes based on the dependencies you must address.

NOTES:

CHAPTER 16 - THE LAST MILE

As the numbers of loose ends begin to pile up, the project seems overwhelming and fatigue begins to set in.

At this point of our journey, it is easy to identify those things that create the plight of a maven. The maven's superpowers of understanding is a path with many challenges. One of the biggest challenges that faces all of us is that of finishing what we start. I, personally, have struggled with this. This is a simple but undisputed concept often overlooked as important and another part of the process. If you are unable to get to the last mile of a project goal or task, this puts the entirety of it in jeopardy.

What keeps us from finishing?

I call this chapter "The Last Mile" because this is the hardest mile of the journey. The same can be said for any project or goal. By the time you get to the last mile, you will be able to see the end, but you are facing some of your biggest challenges yet. If you prioritized things correctly and worked through resolving the dependencies, this mile can be easy, but most of the time you're facing those things that were not obvious. It is a safe bet that all of us have faced a project or a situation where the project was left undone. The real challenge or plight is to keep that situation to a minimum. At the last mile, several things have happened. You have lost your momentum, your priorities have changed, you are fatigued with the project, the resources are running out or scope creep has taken you in directions you did not plan to go.

At this point, you recognize those tools that are available to the maven. In this book I covered a lot of material. Most of the material was geared to the reader in order to unleash the superpowers that came from an enriched understanding. Those powers become tools for success. You may have even been practicing some of these things, which seem like a logical common sense approach. Some will find this very natural. As you will see, these concepts become very important as you reach the last mile of a project or goal.

Keep in mind that success is a journey, not a destination. Just as learning or empowering our understanding in an area of study, the journey is the process. This book tells a story about unleashing your superpowers, there is no success endpoint. Success is what you make of it, or as in a success system, what you described it to be in your success statement.

Knowing when you are finished

In the success systems chapter, I discussed the importance of having a definition of success. This concept becomes important when we are looking for the finish line. In some situations, knowing the finish line is easy or apparent. In a vast majority of projects or goals, not having a clear definition of success will keep you in an endless pursuit of a goal without knowing you finished.

In a baseball game, when the last out of the final ending has been reached, the game is over, but that does not mean your team reached its goal. You may reach the final out of the game and still not win the game; you will not have reached the goal of winning the game. Therefore, having a good bull pen is the key to finishing the game and reaching your teams goals. This is the essence of success. If you never finish a race, you cannot win the race. Finishing is as important as starting. Successful people have the willingness and the ability to finish those things that they start. In some situations, it may no longer be beneficial to finish due to the scope of the project. When a project becomes so overwhelming that the resources required to finish exceed the value gained, the project can and should be scrapped. This is where the tools of the maven become increasingly important.

Watch for the loose ends

Since projects are made up of tasks, it is important to find a way to complete each task. For every task you leave incomplete, that is one more loose end that has to be dealt with. As the numbers of loose ends begin to pile up, the project seems overwhelming and fatigue begins to set in. This is why having a good plan, complete with an understanding of what "finished" looks like is more important than at any other time of the project. I talked about finding your passion; this is when your passion will carry you across the finish line. You may want to call on some other mavens who may be able to provide you with some tips or techniques that will give you the final push. With each project you take on, there are going to be unplanned obstacles. This is where the skills of transferable knowledge will help. You may have encountered a similar problem on a different project, and the way you solved that problem will help on the current project.

Throughout the book, I introduced a number of methods for learning a skill. These methods include recognizing the system, watching for patterns, understanding the patterns, identifying the layers within the system, and, finally, creating options for yourself. These methods are designed to embolden you to not just take on a project, but to complete the project you start. As stated many times, hidden behind the façade of failures are parts of success. By this time, you have encountered some failures, you have used your skills to find options, you studied the system, you recognized patterns and you have made complex problems simpler by breaking the system into layers.

Understanding is your most valuable tool

You may find that you will use all the powers of a maven in order to complete the project. Remember the discussion on tools? Of course you do. We now begin to realize that understanding is a tool. Understanding is a process that is built on a system of learning. Understanding gives us options which, in turn, give us power over situations. You have been given a great and powerful gift as a reader of this book. Your investment of time can now begin to pay off. You may have recognized some of the traits within yourself. You may have been able to figure out if you are an internal or external locus of control individual. You may realize that you need to work on a few areas. You now have a system to use. You can begin using these tools for everything you start and finish. While this book is a very philosophical approach, it is very common sense. It may seem technical at times, but the concepts are simple enough that you can get your mind around them. As you practice these concepts, the way you watch TV will change. You will begin to notice traits in others, both in real life and in fictional books or movies. The way you interact with people (by watching their responses to questions, being able to tell if someone is being honest with you, and by paying attention to patterns) will change. You will want to understand the language of various groups of professionals, and understand exactly what it means. Realizing that there is a motive behind each industry or product, you can learn to find their value. You now understand the reason why learning the history of a product or industry is important. You can begin to craft your own success system by watching the way others have accomplished it. You realize that success is not an accident; it is part of a system. You can have the courage to take on subjects or projects because you know that success will have failures, but those obstacles are part of the process. Dependencies are just something that gives us a priority or a course of action. You can begin to unleash your own superpowers on your path to success.

The plight of the maven is to always learn new things, take on new projects, teach others and extend his or her capabilities.

NOTES:

ABOUT THE AUTHOR

Most young men growing up in rural communities learn how to fix farm equipment because it's a necessity to get the work done. Having grown up in a small South Texas town, Wesley Crenshaw Jr.'s first mechanic experience was keeping his families lawn mower running. It was not all work and no play though; growing up in the country also meant riding motorcycles in the wide open spaces. This required him to learn to work on them as well to keep them running. He soon was recruited by his friends to fix theirs as well.

Wesley's first job at the age of 14 was working in the town's only auto parts store. There he was exposed to all things automotive: cars, tractors, and motorcycles. He gained an understanding of business at an early age. He was machining parts and rebuilding engines before he was even in high school.

Wesley gained more skills in drafting, physics, and metallurgy in his high school and college years. Those combined with his already well-honed mechanical skills, opened all types of possibilities. Those combined skills set the stage for his first real career as a tool and die maker.

Wesley worked as a tool and die maker for a small manufacturing company, designing and building tools to produce various types of parts from various materials. While there, he taught himself computer programming, this for him, as a "tool maker," seemed a natural step. Computers offered him a whole new world of challenges and tool building opportunities.

The management knew they needed some automation. The available technology was expensive and they struggled with trusting and understanding it. In the end the cost could not be justified.

Wesley's understanding of the technology allowed him to develop needed solutions for the shop. Initially his ideas were rejected by management because they did not understand them. The VP of production finally relented and bought him a programmable calculator for the shop. When Wes wrote programs to calculate material yields and solve design issues the VP was able to prove it worked and management starting seeing the value of computerized automation with Wesley leading the way.

Wesley became the point person for choosing, purchasing, and setting up the needed equipment for their first CAD system. He moved into designing the tools and programming the CAD system to automate that process. Based on the strength of his abilities, the company began buying sophisticated CNC machines and put Wesley in charge of the programming department.

At a time before networking computers was common, Wesley grew with the technology and learned to network all the company computer systems together to share information. As computer systems became more capable he was able to get more solutions out of them. Wesley soon found himself writing custom programs and software tools that were incorporated into the company's UNIX system. Wesley expanded his understanding of the midrange system and began finding more uses for the platforms.

In the mid 1990's, Wesley was sought out by an IT Manager for a Fortune 100 Company which has one of the largest IT departments in the country with data centers all over the U.S. and Europe. He went to work there as an automation developer. His programming code was now running on thousands of UNIX and Windows platforms all over the country.

Wesley wrote this book to share with others how you can learn to understand systems in a way that would allow you to unleash your superpowers.

AUTHOR WESLEY V. CRENSHAW JR.

ACKNOWLEDGMENTS

I want to thank my wife Vickie Collie Crenshaw for all her help in proof reading and being a sounding board for me during the writing of this book. I acknowledge that since we both have various ways of looking as things, her assistance was crucial in articulating the messages in this text. I want to also acknowledge her patience and persistence that gave me the motivation to complete this project when other priorities kept getting in the way. I want to thank my parents, whom were the first people in my life to draw inspiration from. My mom gave me skill of being a craftsman and my dad gave me the gift of insight and vision. Both allowed me to grow into who I am.

I want to thank my first wife, Angela Colbert, whose presence in my life was responsible for helping me become who I became. She was there through the early years becoming a maven in her own right; she would recognize that we grew into this together. She was also the one who helped me raise two wonderful sons, who have become wonderful young men and are currently experiencing the fruits of being raised as mavens.

I have to give a special thank you to Debra Englander of Steve Harrison's Quantum Leap program for her experience. Debra proofread my original manuscript and was brutally honest with the changes that needed to be made, this lead to a re-write that helped produce a better book.

Thank you to Shain Clark who edited the final version of the manuscript. Her experience as an English teacher gave this book a professional touch.

Thank you to Robert Inman my chef friend who sat with me and helped me formulate a number of concepts in this book. Robert was a key contributor to the outline of the success system. Robert's stories of his own experiences dovetail with my own to reinforce the points in this book.

Thank you to the late Sid Tanner. Sid was the VP at the company where I honed many of my skills. It was his positive support and honest skepticism that helped me understand the skills necessary.

This is a thank you to all my friends, those who allowed me to teach them and others who I drew inspiration from by watching the way they took on problems and solved them. There is a special thank you to the friends whose problems I solved and gave me the reinforcement to build my own confidence.